Les Recettes de la Saison

Les Recettes de la Saison

A Holiday Cookbook from

Les Chefs de la Madeleine

and

Susan Herrmann Loomis

Copyright

Published by la Madeleine, Inc.

Photographer: Gus Schmiege
Food Stylist: Brooke Leonard
Editor: Kathy A. Dubé
Art Director & Photo Stylist: Noëlle LeDoux
Graphic Coordinator: Alison Daffin Schmiege
Initial Concepts: Larry Reinschmidt and Kirk Massey
Contributing Writers: Poppy Sundeen and Bunny Polmer

Manufactured in the United States
Imprimé aux Etats Unis

Acknowledgements
Nos Remerciements

Photography	Gustav Schmiege
Food Styling	Brooke Leonard
Editor	Kathy A. Dubé
Art Director & Photo Stylist	Noëlle LeDoux
Graphic Coordinator	Alison Daffin Schmiege
Initial Concepts	Larry Reinschmidt Kirk Massey
Contributing Writers	Poppy Sundeen Bunny Polmer
Final Layout, Color & Pre-press	Composite Color

Merci Beaucoup

Many thanks to the following people, without whom
this cookbook would not have been so successful.

Photo location hosts
Beverly and Ray Morrison
Jan Barboglio

The grande family of la Madeleine recipe testers.
A special thank you to John Carino, for all of his contributions to
Les Recettes de la Saison.
ur special thanks to Ryan Thrash for enduring the journey to creative perfection.

Guest Forum participants
Darlene Ballarini, Cheryl Weatherly Binnie, Bonnie Blesse, Charmaine Driver,

Kay Frierson, Anna Lee Harris, Anne-Claude Leridée-Nance, Sandy C. Massman,

Betty W. Rush, Jean Dunlap Wallace

Table of Contents
Table des Matièrs

Les Legumes
Vegetables

Green Beans with Almonds and Tomatoes, 46
Carrot and Butternut Squash Soufflé, 48
Cranberry, Raspberry and Orange Relish, 49
Mushroom Duxelle, 49
Spinach with Cream, 50
Chestnuts and Red Cabbage, 50
Potato Gratin, 52
Mashed Potatoes and Celery Root, 54
la Madeleine Seven Grain Stuffing, 55

Les Desserts et les Pains
Desserts & Breads

Holiday Cookies, 60
Linzer Cookies, 62
Almond Tuiles, 63
Pain d'Épices, 64
Stollen, 65
Mixed Berry Tart, 66
Lavender Honey Crème Brûlée, 68
Chocolate Charlotte, 69
Chocolate Darioles, 70
Tarte Tatin, 72
Roasted Apples, 75
Christmas Log, 76
King's Cake, 79
Pascal's Pumpkin Cheesecake, 80
Almond Tart Dough, 81
Brioche, 82
Old World Baguette, 84
Feuilletage Dough, 86

La Belle France

La Manche

Nord Pas de Calais

La Belgique

Luxembourg

Aisne

L'Allem

Picardie

Normandie

Champagne Ardenne

Lorraine

Bretagne

Ile de France

Alsac

Pays de La Loire

Franche Comté

Centre Val de Loire

Bourgogne

La Sui

L'Atlantic

Poitou Charentes

Limousin

Auvergne

Rhone Alpes

Golfe de Gascogne

Aquitaine

L'I

Midi Pyrenees

Côte d'Azur

Provence

Languedoc Roussillon

L'Espagne

Mer Mediterranée

Introduction

There is a heightened merriment at la Madeleine before and during the holidays. At this time of the year, you will find friends chatting over coffee and pastries and families laughing over dinner before the out-of town relatives descend upon them. You will see la Madeleine associates relishing in our guests' delight and truly enjoying the Gallic air which is crackling with excitement.

La Madeleine is pleased to be part of the good cheer and celebration of the thousands of guests who pass through our doors during the holiday season and throughout the year. Since 1983, we have been part of our guest's lives, their "home away from home." From the moment we opened our first bakery, we have been carefully listening to our guests' needs and interests, adapting to and surprising them.

At first, we simply baked genuine French breads and pastries. Soon we added soups, salads and delicious sandwiches. Next, we provided an assortment of French country recipes and seasonal specialties like the ones we hand-picked for this book. Along the way, guests clamored for us to bottle their favorite soups and salad dressings. Later, we added a retail line of ceramics and unique, French-inspired gifts. Still, we receive many, many requests for our recipes and more knowledge of the French country culture.

We are proud to share some French holiday secrets, flavors and specialties with you. At la Madeleine, the holiday season starts with Thanksgiving, continues through Christmas and New Year's Day and ends with the Feast of the Epiphany. We believe you will enjoy the journey as you explore our roots, traditions and family recipes. Some of the recipes came to us on well-worn pieces of paper passed down from generation to generation. Others have incorporated more modern twists. All of the recipes are a part of our Chefs' "Favorites" file. They are tried-and-true, simple to prepare and enormously satisfying. From hot, comforting soups and lively party favorites to seasonal entrées and magnifique pâtisseries, all will truly enjoy these foods in the best of French traditions. We hope that you will turn to **Les Recettes de la Saison** when you want to recreate an authentic French country experience in your own home.
As always, bon appétit!

Jour de Grace

Thanksgiving Dinner

Entrée
Soupe à la Crème de Champignons Grillés

Plats de Resistance
Dinde Rotie avec Farce aux Sept Graines
Purée de Pommes de Terre et Céleri Rave
Coulis de Canneberges, Framboises et Orange
Soufflé de Carotte et de Courgette

Salade
Mesclun à la Vinaigrette à l'Echalotte

Fromage au Choix

Vin
Bourgogne

Desserts & Café
Gateau au Fromage Blanc et au Potiron
Pommes au Four

Menu de Noël

Christmas Dinner

Pour Commencer
Champagne et Huitres en Fête

Entrée
Soupe à l'Oignon avec Croutons au Fromage

Plats de Resistance
Boeuf en Croûte avec une Duxelle de Champignon
Haricots Verts aux Amandes et à la Tomate
Pommes de Terre au Gratin

Salade
Salade d'Endives

Fromage au Choix

Vin
Bordeaux

Dessert & Café
Bûche de Noël

Cocktail de la Saint Sylvestre

New Year's Eve Cocktail

Apéritifs
Champagne Chambord
Vin Chaud
Vin à l'Orange

Les Hors d'Oeuvres
Pain Surprise
Bâtons au Fromage et au Pesto
Crevettes Enrubannes de Lard Fumé
Canapés au Saumon Fumé
Amandes au Sel Marin et au Thym

Les Desserts
Petits Gâteaux de Fête
Les Tartelettes Linzer
Tuiles aux Amandes

Menu de l'Epiphanie

Epiphany Dinner

Entrée
Salade Mesclun au Foie Gras

Plats de Résistance
Gigot d'Agneau à la Mirepoix
Pommes de Terre au Gratin
Châtaignes et Chou Rouge

Salade
Salade à la Vinaigrette à l'Echalotte

Fromage
Brie, Pont l'Évêque, Chèvre

Vin
Bordeaux

Dessert & Café
Galettes des Rois

Les Vins

Olives	Côtes de Provence
Oysters	Champagne
Goat Cheese	Sancerre, Pinot Blanc
Smoked Salmon	Champagne
Foie Gras	Sauternes, Chinon
Salad	Sauvignon, Chardonnay
Shellfish	Côtes du Rhône, Pouilly Fuissé
Fish	Côtes du Rhône, Pouilly Fumé
Red Meats	Chateâuneuf du Pape, Paulliac, Marguax
Poultry	St Émilion, St. Estéphe
Desserts	Champagne, Sauternes, Vouvray
Cheeses	Côtes du Rhône

Susan Herrmann Loomis

Internationally known journalist, chef and cookbook author Susan Herrmann Loomis is an expert on food. During her extensive travels throughout the United States, France and Italy, she has met with all types of people – from farmers to merchants to commercial fishermen. In meeting these people, Susan has used her journalistic training to investigate the entire world of food. In doing so, she has learned about the morés, customs and beliefs of countries and their regions, and she has infused her work with lively anecdotes and keen insights about the people she has met.

Susan Herrmann Loomis has been a key element in maintaining our French roots by introducing our general managers to the heritage of French country cooking. Twice a year new general managers go to France to learn about the food, culture and traditions of France. Loomis hosts the managers at her home in Normandy where they discover many aspects of life in the French countryside. Susan Herrmann Loomis also consulted on the conception and realization of this book.

Loomis has appeared as a guest on many radio and television stations in the U.S. and France, including National Public Radio and Good Morning America in the U.S., and FR3 and Radio Bleu in France. She is a consultant for British publisher Weidenfield & Nicolson, and she is the weekly columnist for CONDENAST ONLINE (www.food.epicurious.com) where her Letter from France appears each week.

Loomis began her writing career in newspapers in Washington state, and moved from there to Paris where she attended the renowned culinary school, La Varenne École de Cuisine. With a Grand Diplome from there in hand, Loomis opened a small café in Paris where she cooked for a year, before launching a successful writing career.

Currently a resident of France, Loomis makes her home in Louviers, Normandy, with her husband, Michael, their nine-year old son, Joseph and seven-month old daughter, Fiona.

la Madeleine Chefs

Remy Schaal, Corporate Executive Chef and Director of Product Development, started his career at la Madeleine as a baker but quickly grew into the role of chef, food purveyor and head of product and menu development for la Madeleine.

Remy's roots are deep in Alsace, where his parents grew their own food, pressed their own wine and where his uncle ran the local pastry and bakery shop. As a young boy, Remy worked in his uncle's shop. At the age of sixteen, he began to train formally, concentrating on fine specialty cakes. After completing his "Brevet de Compagnons", his travels took him throughout France, from Paris and Chamonix to Reims, Champagne and Strasbourg, working and gathering ideas. After working in Nancy and Alsace, which is also the home of his wife, Remy came to Dallas in 1984 to work for la Madeleine.

For fifteen years Remy has been instrumental in helping la Madeleine preserve its French authenticity. He travels back to France at least twice a year to meet with French chefs, attend French food shows and explore French recipes and ingredients. He oversees how our traditional French artisanship blends with contemporary American taste. Remy also recruits and mentors the talented French chefs that have made la Madeleine what it is today. When he is not crafting new exciting dishes he can be seen on morning talk shows and cooking shows and heard on radio programs around the country. Remy is a rare chef that cooks with his heart and he has encouraged that quality in each of the la Madeleine chefs.

Frederic Cordier, Head Chef in Phoenix, is a native of Buxy in the Burgundy region of France. Apprenticed at the age of fifteen, Frederic mastered the art of both boulangerie and pâtisserie by working for bakers in his village. After a stint in the French army and a job at a ski resort, he headed for the Montpelier Hotel in Verbier, Switzerland, where he became the baker. From here, Frederic headed to Fife, Scotland where he worked as a chef de pâtisserie.

To escape the cold of his new residence, he took a two week vacation to Dallas to visit his brother. He was immediately pleased with the warmer climate. While in

la Madeleine Chefs

Dallas, he learned about la Madeleine and enthusiastically moved to Phoenix to help open our new bakeries. Four years later, he heads up the Phoenix kitchen and has done a outstanding job. The Arizona Republic's entertainment guide, The Rep's Best, named la Madeleine's pastries the best in Phoenix.

Serge Faucon, one of la Madeleine's chefs, traces his love of bread to his childhood in Le Creusot, a village in Burgundy. He remembers walking past the town bakery when he was eleven, savoring the smell and wishing he could be the one to pull out the billowy loaves from the big, wood burning oven.

Convincing his father that bread baking was his calling, Serge began as an apprentice in boulangerie and pâtisserie when he was fifteen years old. For two years he worked at the local bakery and attended pastry school, earning his certificate. He was also a finalist in a national competition with his decorative and artisan breads.

Three years later, after serving in the army and several jobs, Serge was introduced to la Madeleine and Remy Schaal by his brother, a chef, who was living in Houston. By 1994 the paperwork was in progress, and a year later Serge was on board at la Madeleine.

Though his experience at la Madeleine has taken him through all aspects of food production, it is still bread which claims his heart and soul. It must be hereditary, even his three-year-old daughter Madeleine has a favorite: pumpkin cheesecake.

Pascal Ginepio, Corporate Boulangerie Chef, comes from a family of bakers. Born in Marseille and raised in Nice, Pascal learned boulangerie and pâtisserie from his father, in his three star restaurant and bakery. By the time he was fourteen, he was proficient in pastry making, bread baking and viennoisserie.

After earning a degree in interior design and working for his uncle, an architect, Pascal took a break to travel the world. Enticed by opportunities he found in the United States, Pascal worked as a bread consultant in Boston and Dallas and opened his own bakery in San Francisco. After helping open la Madeleine's location in Dallas, Pascal joined the company's corporate team.

Les Hors d'Oeuvre et Apéritifs

Appetizers & Apéritifs

Pain Surprise

Kalamata Olive Tapenade

Olive Pesto Cheese Bâtons

Oysters en Fête

Goat Cheese Canapés

Bacon Wrapped Shrimp

Smoked Salmon Canapés

Almonds with Sea Salt and Thyme

Ham & Asparagus Canapés

Champagne Chambord

Vin Chaud

Vin à l'Orange

Pain Surprise

4 lb. Miche, rye or wheat

2 sticks unsalted butter

3 tablespoons Dijon mustard

½ cup cornichons,
finely chopped

¼ pound ham, sliced

¼ pound smoked turkey, sliced

¼ pound Gruyère, sliced

¼ pound Rosette de Lyon
salami, sliced

Pain Surprise
Pain Surprise

No party in France is complete without a pain surprise, a rustic loaf that is hollowed out, it's crumb kept intact; sliced, then filled with savory fillings and cut into finger sandwiches. The sandwiches are then carefully fitted back into the loaf. Fillings can vary. We offer several here that have proven, time and again, to be favorites with both adults and children. In our recipe, the sandwiches made with ham, turkey and Gruyère particularly appeal to children. The others, those with herbs, capers and Roquefort, are more sophisticated, appealing in general to more adult palates.

In France, bakers prefer using bread that is a day old, for its crumb holds together well. However, you may use fresh bread, although it will be somewhat more difficult to remove the crumb. Should you find yourself lacking in crumb for the sandwiches, simply buy another loaf of bread and use it as a complement.

Cut the top of the Miche to form a lid. Set aside.

Carefully hollow out and remove the "crumb" of the bread in one piece by carefully slicing with a serrated knife around the inside edge of the loaf. To cut along the bottom, insert a sharp knife into the bread on one side about ¼ inch from the bottom without making a large slice in the side of the loaf. Move the knife blade so that you are slicing along the bottom of the loaf to separate the crumb from the crust, reaching in as far as you can. Insert the knife on the other side of the bread and repeat. Repeat on yet another side of the bread if necessary, to make sure that the "crumb" is completely separated from the crust.

Set the hollowed out bread and the lid aside, as you will use it later. Take the crumb and slice horizontally into 8 thin slices. Soften the butter. Add the mustard and cornichons and mix until thoroughly combined. Spread the butter mixture on one side of a slice, lay a slice of ham atop it, and spread another slice with the butter mixture. Set the other slice, butter-side down, atop the ham pressing down, gently. Spread the remaining slices on one side with the butter mixture, and top them with the remaining meats and cheese. Stack the sandwiches and cut the stack into 12 triangles.

Pain Surprise (suite)

Pain Surprise

Pain Surprise

Pain Surprise Fillings

2 sticks unsalted butter, softened

1 tablespoon fresh tarragon, minced

1 tablespoon capers, drained and minced

1 ½ teaspoons Roquefort

2 fresh sage leaves, minced

pinch sea salt

Divide the butter into 4 equal parts and place in small bowls. Add the tarragon to the butter in one bowl, the capers to another. Add the Roquefort to the third bowl of butter and the sage and sea salt to the fourth. Mix well to form a smooth paste. Make four sandwiches by spreading the different mixtures on one side of each of the four slices of bread (one per side) and topping each with a slice of bread. Cut each into triangles. Stack the sandwiches and cut into 12 triangles.

Place the entire stack of sandwiches inside the crust, they will rise slightly above the edge of the bread. To present your pain surprise, cock the top of the loaf atop the sandwiches — which will come slightly above the edge of the bread — and tie it up with brightly colored ribbon.

Serves 8

Seven grain or whole wheat breads add flavor and interest.

Kalamata Olive Tapenade

Tapenade d'Olives Kalamata

In the Mediterranean, olive trees transform the hillsides into a gorgeous, silvery green. Olives are a way of life in this rustic area, where they are pressed for oil or ground with herbs and spices into tapenade. Winter is olive season and the minute the olives are harvested and cured, fresh tapenade makes its appearance in market, sold in huge flat bowls. The appearance of the year's first olives and tapenades makes a wonderful excuse for festivities to begin.

Tapenade makes a lovely savory appetizer either spread on toast, as indicated, or used as a dip with fresh vegetables. Vary this by adding minced fresh basil or thyme.

Soak the anchovies in white wine to cover for 20 minutes to remove the salt. Drain and pat dry.

Using a food processor, combine the oil, capers, olives, anchovies and garlic. Puree to a thick, rough paste.

Remove the outer crust from the brioche slices, cut each slice into 4 equal pieces and toast in a 325° oven until golden. Using a small spoon or rubber spatula spread 1 teaspoon of the tapenade on each brioche crouton.

Garnish each canape with a sprig of parsley, arrange on a platter and serve immediately.

Makes 32 canapés

Kalamata Olive Tapenade

6 anchovy fillets

1 tablespoon extra virgin
olive oil

1 tablespoon capers

2 cups Kalamata olives, pitted

1 small clove garlic

8 slices brioche
(see page 82)

parsley sprigs for garnish

Anchovy paste can be substituted for anchovy filets.

Olive Pesto Cheese Bâtons

¾ cup Kalamata olives, pitted

1 tablespoon capers, rinsed & drained

3 tablespoons olive oil

1 tablespoon fresh lemon juice

¼ teaspoon fresh thyme leaves, firmly packed.

ground black pepper, to taste.

1 pound Feuilletage Dough (page86) or frozen puff pastry dough, thawed

2 cups Swiss, grated

Olive Pesto Cheese Bâton
Bâtons au Fromage et au Pesto

No one can resist these satisfyingly crisp "straws" which are rich with olive flavor and heightened by the accent of capers. Best when served warm, these are ideal to serve before a celebratory holiday meal, preferably with a glass of chilled champagne.

Place all the ingredients (excluding the feuilletage dough and Swiss cheese) in a blender or a food processor fitted with the metal blade. Pulse on and off until it forms a rough textured purée.

On a lightly floured surface roll out the dough into a rectangle about 16 inches long, 7 inches wide, and 1⁄16 inch thick. Facing the long side of the rectangle spread the pesto sauce over the dough.

Sprinkle the Swiss cheese evenly over the pesto. With a sharp knife or pizza cutter cut 16 strips 1 inch thick.

Place on a baking sheet lined with parchment paper. Leave about 1 inch between the straws or they will stick to each other.

Let rest in the refrigerator for 1 hour prior to baking. Bake for 10 to 15 minutes at 450°.

Serve warm.

Makes 16

To make classic cheese bâtons, eliminate the pesto.

Oysters "en fête"

¼ cup unsalted butter, softened

¼ cup flat leaf parsley

1 clove garlic, minced

½ tablespoon of fresh
lemon juice

¼ teaspoon of salt

Pinch of freshly ground pepper

16 oysters on the half shell

Oysters
"Mignonette Sauce"

¼ cup red wine vinegar

1 small shallot, finely chopped

Cracked black pepper, to taste

Oysters en Fête

Huîtres en Fête

The French consume literally tons of oysters each year at Christmas and New Year's. In the French view, oysters are essential for closing the year, perhaps because they are thought to be not only good for you, but also restorative and filled with energy. Certainly they are all that but mostly they are delicious.

The most popular way to eat oysters in France is raw, on the half shell, usually accompanied by a mignonette sauce and thin slices of fresh bread slathered with unsalted butter. Here we offer a little something extra, oysters that are heated just long enough to melt the savory garlic butter.

Garlic Butter

In a small bowl combine the softened butter with the minced parsley, garlic and lemon juice. Season with salt and pepper.

Arrange the oysters on a baking pan and top each with 1 teaspoon of the flavored butter.

Place the oysters 3 inches from the broiler element and broil until the butter is melted and bubbling and the oysters are hot, about 3 minutes. Serve immediately.

Serves 4

Mignonette Sauce

Combine the vinegar, shallots and pepper and refrigerate for 2 hours. Place oysters on a platter of chipped ice. Serve the mignonette sauce on the side.

Serves 4

The freshest oysters smell of the sea.

Goat Cheese Canapés

Canapés au Fromage de Chèvre

These light lovely little canapés, with their creamy cheese brightened by fresh chives, appeal to everyone. They seem to disappear as fast as they emerge from the oven. Serve them warm when their fresh herbed flavor is at its peak. These may be used as a topping on the classic French salad, Chèvre Chaud.

Lightly toast the baguette slices on one side in a 350° oven until golden brown.

Place the cheese, egg yolks and pepper into a food processor and process until well mixed. Mince the chives and fold into the mixture by hand.

Whisk the egg whites with a pinch of salt until they have formed soft peaks. Fold them into the goat cheese mixture. Using a pastry tube with a star tip, pipe equal amount of filling on the untoasted side of the baguette, (about 2 tablespoons per slice) or you may simply place a dollop of filling onto each slice of baguette using a teaspoon.

Bake in a preheated 425° oven until the cheese is golden, about ten minutes. Garnish each canape with the pointed tip of a chive and serve immediately.

Makes 24 canapés

Goat Cheese Canapés

24 pieces of baguette,
sliced into ½ inch slices

1 pound of soft goat cheese
such as Montrachet

2 eggs, separated

½ teaspoon black pepper

2 tablespoons chives, diced

Make sure to use soft French goat cheese in this recipe.

Bacon Wrapped Shrimp

Bacon Wrapped Shrimp

24 pieces shrimp, 21-25 count

3 tablespoons Holiday Seasoning

12 strips bacon, cut in half

Roasted Pepper Mayonnaise

½ cup roasted red peppers, jarred

½ cup Boursin

½ cup cream cheese

¼ cup crème fraiche

¼ teaspoon black pepper

1 tablespoon fresh basil, chopped

sea salt, to taste

Holiday Seasoning

1 cup dried orange peel

½ cup whole fennel seed

½ cup lemon pepper

¼ cup sea salt

2 tablespoons dried lemon peel

3 tablespoons garlic powder

Bacon Wrapped Shrimp

Crevettes Enrubannées de Lard Fumé

Inspired by John Carino, these spicy shrimp wrapped in thin bacon slices make any holiday soirée extra special. Simple to make, quick to cook, they emerge from the broiler tender and juicy. Be sure to use very thinly sliced bacon so that it cooks and crisps quickly.

Roll the shrimp in the holiday seasoning, wrap each shrimp with a half-slice of bacon and secure with a toothpick.

Place onto a baking pan. Bake at 350° for 8 to 10 minutes. Turn the shrimp over halfway through the cooking time so that the bacon cooks evenly.

Serve with roasted pepper mayonnaise.

Makes 24 shrimp

Roasted Pepper Mayonnaise

Place the roasted red peppers into a food processor and puree. Add the Boursin and the cream cheese, and process until well combined.

Add the crème fraiche, black pepper, basil and sea salt, mix for 10 seconds. Remove and refrigerate.

Makes 1 ½ cups

Holiday Seasoning

Mix all the ingredients together in a small bowl.

Makes 2½ cups

Try this with different flavors of bacon.

Smoked Salmon Canapés

Canapés au Saumon Fumé

In France, smoked salmon is synonymous with a festive occasion, whether it is Christmas, Easter, or simply a fête to celebrate the end of the school year. Here, it is the star of a simple, but delicious and very satisfying mouthful. The salmon also lends lively color to any appetizer offering. The ideal drink for smoked salmon canapés? Champagne, of course!

Smoked Salmon Canapés

6 slices of brioche
approx. 4"x 4" square
(see page 82)

2 tablespoons unsalted butter, softened

½ pound smoked salmon,
thinly sliced

1 small bunch dill or fennel sprigs

2 tablespoons capers

Cut the brioche into any shape you like with a cookie cutter, or simply cut the brioche into triangles. Toast in a 325° oven until golden.

Spread a thin layer of butter on each piece.

Twist the salmon slices and place on the toast.

Decorate with dill and capers.

Serve chilled.

Makes 24 canapés

Almonds with Sea Salt and Thyme

Amandes au Sel Marin et au Thym

Almonds with Sea Salt and Thyme

3 tablespoons unsalted butter

2 cups almonds

½ teaspoon fine sea salt or to taste

2 tablespoons fresh thyme leaves

Toasty and herb laced, these almonds are a hit at any party; the perfect nibble with a chilled cocktail, a glass of Vin à l'Orange or Champagne. They are delicious right after they are made, and they will stay fresh in an airtight container for at least one week.

Heat the butter in a skillet over medium heat. Add the almonds and cook, stirring constantly, until they begin to turn golden brown and give off a toasty smell, about 10 minutes. Remove from the heat. Sprinkle generously with salt and the fresh thyme, tossing the almonds so they are thoroughly coated and all the ingredients are combined. Let cool until slightly warmer than room temperature, and serve.

Makes 2 cups

Fleur de Sel, from Guérande, is the *Sel de la Sel*!

Ham & Asparagus Canapés

Canapés au Jambon et aux Asperges

This is a simple, elegant canapé often served with a glass of champagne or holiday spirits at parties. The technique illustrated here can be adapted for many canapé combinations. Try experimenting with ideas of your own.

Toast the slice of brioche in a 325° oven until golden. Spread the butter on the brioche slices.

Cover each slice with ham. Cut in four squares and place an asparagus tip on each square.

Using a pastry brush carefully spread warm aspic on each canapé to coat the entire surface.

Chill in refrigerator until ready to serve.

Makes 32 canapés

Aspic

Mix the contents of one gelatin package with the beef stock. Bring to a boil. Let the mixture cool slightly and then add the brandy or port.

Makes 1 cup

Ham & Asparagus Canapés

8 slices of brioche (see page 82)
or good quality bread

½ stick unsalted butter, softened

½ pound ham, sliced

24 asparagus tips,
steamed until tender crisp

½ cup aspic

Aspic

1 package unflavored gelatin

1 cup beef stock

½ teaspoon brandy or port

Use a spray bottle to evenly coat the canapés with aspic.

Champagne Chambord

4 tablespoons Chambord liqueur

4 teaspoons fresh lemon juice

One bottle of "brut" Champagne, chilled

24 fresh raspberries

Vin Chaud

½ cups water

2 tablespoons granulated sugar

1 bottle dry red table wine

One cinnamon stick

One star anise

4 lemon slices

4 orange slices

Champagne Chambord
Champagne Chambord

True Champagne is the sparkling wine produced only in the Champagne region of France, near the cities of Reims and Epernay. First enjoyed by the French royals in the early 18th century, it soon became the drink of choice for special celebrations, fêtes and holidays. The addition of Chambord, France's famous raspberry liqueur, adds an even more festive note to the occasion.

Fill each Champagne flute with 1 tablespoon Chambord liqueur and 1 teaspoon fresh lemon juice. Pour the Champagne into the flute. Top each flute with raspberries.

Serve immediately.

Serves 4

Vin Chaud
Vin Chaud

Reflecting on childhood, Chef Remy Schaal was happy to share a special memory of winter. He, and the other men in the family, would spend the chilly day working in the family's vineyards. They would return hungry and cold but happy to be greeted with cups full of warm spiced wine which was served by the blazing fire.

In a saucepan, combine the water and the sugar and bring to a boil. Add the red wine, cinnamon and star anise and let simmer for 5 minutes. Remove from the heat, add the lemon and orange slices and let macerate for 15 minutes. Remove the spices and the lemon and orange slices. Serve warm

Serves 4

Pinot Noir is the signature wine of Alsace.

Vin à l'Orange

Vin à l'Orange

12 large oranges,
preferably organic or untreated

2 bottles of white wine,
such as Sancerre or Pinot Blanc

2 cups of vodka

1 vanilla bean, scored down
its length

2 ¼ cups sugar, divided in half

This lovely, aromatic aperitif is made throughout France in winter, when oranges are at their prime. It is most often drunk in the winter soon after it is made, around a cozy fire, in celebration of a fine day on the ski slopes. Some people turn this tradition around, however, by letting it age in the bottle for six months and serving slightly chilled in summer, when oranges are simply a memory but their perfume is a welcome treat.

Peel the oranges right down to the fruit, including the pith. Put the fruit aside for another use.

Place the skins and the pith in a large, non-reactive pot or bowl. Add the wine, vodka, vanilla bean and half the sugar. Stir.

Caramelize the remaining sugar in a small, heavy saucepan over medium-high heat. The sugar will melt and begin to bubble then gradually liquefy, turning a golden color, which will take about 7 minutes. Continue cooking, swirling the pan, until the caramel is a deep golden color, about 5 minutes. Do not stir.

Remove the pan from the heat and pour the caramelized sugar into the orange mixture, scraping as much of the sugar from the pan with a wooden spoon as possible.

The caramel will sizzle and send up steam, and will harden instantly, then gradually melt into the wine. Stir, cover, and let sit for 72 hours.

Strain the wine through a sieve lined with two thicknesses of cheesecloth, into sterilized bottles. Seal with corks and let sit for at least 3 weeks and up to one year before drinking.

To avoid pesticides, use organic oranges if possible.

Les Notes

Les Entrées
Starters

Onion Soup and Cheese Croutons

Cream of Turnip Soup

Roasted Mushroom Soup

Endive Salad

Wild Field Greens with Foie Gras

Onion Soup and Cheese Croutons

Soupe à l'Oignon avec Croutons au Fromage

Onion Soup & Cheese Croutons

3 tablespoons unsalted butter

3 tablespoons olive oil

¾ pound yellow onions, sliced

¾ pound purple onions, sliced

1 teaspoon sea salt

1 tablespoon cracked black pepper

¼ cup sherry

1 tablespoon brandy

1 quart beef stock

1 bay leaf

4 sprigs fresh thyme

1 baguette, sliced 1-inch thick

⅔ cup Gruyère, grated

Onion soup is a specialty at French fêtes, when it is traditionally eaten during the wee morning hours after an evening of festivities. The late night revelers enjoy a steaming bowl of onion soup that has sat for a day to deepen and develop its flavors.

You needn't wait until 3:00 a.m. to enjoy this flavorful soup – make it for any chilly winter evening or any time you feel like a wonderful bowl of soup. You may also stir the cheese into the soup rather than grilling it atop the croutons.

Place the butter and the oil in a large saucepan over medium heat. When the butter melts and begins to foam, add the onions. Cook for about 20 minutes, covered, until the onions are tender and a pale golden brown. Season lightly with salt and pepper. Add the sherry and the brandy, stir and cook for 4 minutes. Add the stock, bay leaf and thyme and bring to a boil over medium heat. Reduce the heat so the liquid simmers and continue cooking, covered, for at least 25 minutes. Brush the baguette slices with olive oil and toast until golden brown to make croutons.

Divide the soup among warmed soup bowls. Place a crouton on top of each bowl of soup and cover with an equal amount of cheese. Place under a preheated broiler until the cheese is melted and bubbling, 3 to 5 minutes. Serve immediately.

Serves 4

Use Gruyère for an authentic French taste.

Cream of Turnip Soup

2 tablespoons unsalted butter

1 large yellow onion, sliced

1 pound turnips,
peeled and diced

1 ½ quarts chicken stock

1 teaspoon salt

1 teaspoon cracked
black pepper

½ cup whipping cream

Chervil or parsley for garnish

Cream of Turnip Soup

Soupe à la Crème et Navet

Turnips have never tasted as delicious as they do in this soup! In the fall, when turnips have sweetened during the first frost, this makes a lovely dish to celebrate the changing of the seasons. Be sure to serve this soup piping hot in an elegant setting — it deserves nothing less.

Melt the butter over medium heat in a large saucepan. When the butter is melted, add the onions and cook, stirring until the onions begin to soften, about 4 minutes. Add the turnips, stir and cook until they start to turn golden, about 10 minutes. Pour in the the chicken stock and season with salt and pepper.

Cover the saucepan and bring to a boil. Immediately reduce the heat until the stock is at a lively simmer and cook until the turnips are tender, about 1 hour. Remove from the heat and puree with a wand mixer or a food processor. Whisk in the cream, adjust the seasoning and place over medium heat until the soup is hot. Be careful not to let the soup boil.

Divide the soup among 4 soup bowls. Garnish with herbs and serve.

Serves 4

Try turnips in a gratin, mashed or in a salad.

Roasted Mushroom Soup
Soupe à la Crème de Champignons Grillés

This soup is simultaneously hearty and elegant. It is a wonderful celebration of Spring and Fall, seasons when the French take to the woods to harvest an abundance of wild mushrooms. The locations of mushroom beds are closely guarded and practically sacred, handed down from generation to generation.

This recipe calls for chanterelles and porcini (bolete) mushrooms, as well as common button mushrooms. If you can't find either the chanterelles or the boletes, substitute an equal amount of other varieties of wild mushrooms for equally delicious results.

Clean the mushrooms by either brushing with a mushroom brush or gently wiping with a damp cloth.

Place mushrooms and ¼ cup of the olive oil into a large baking pan. Toss well. Bake at 375° for 20 minutes.

Place a large saucepan over medium heat, and add the remaining olive oil, butter, roasted mushrooms and sherry. Cook for 2 minutes, then stir in the thyme and black pepper.

Sprinkle flour over the mushrooms and stir. Stir in the stock, salt and bay leaves. Bring to boil and reduce the heat to a simmer. Simmer for 35 minutes or until the soup gives off a rich smell. Remove the bay leaves. Puree the mixture in a food processor or blender.

Just before serving whisk in the cream. Warm the soup over low heat until it is hot and steaming, but do not boil. Adjust the seasonings to taste and serve.

Serves 4

Roasted Mushroom Soup

1 pound button mushrooms

½ pound chanterelle mushrooms

½ pound porcini or bolete mushrooms

¼ cup plus 2 tablespoons olive oil

¼ cup unsalted butter

2 tablespoons sherry

4 sprigs fresh thyme

coarsely ground black pepper, to taste

¼ cup flour

2 quarts chicken stock

sea salt, to taste

2 bay leaves

1 cup heavy cream

You can substitute dried mushrooms for variety.

Endive Salad

2 medium pears, peeled and cored

1 tablespoon freshly squeezed lemon juice

1 pound endive, trimmed

4 ounces Roquefort cheese

½ cup walnut halves, lightly toasted

Shallot Vinaigrette

sea salt, to taste

freshly ground pepper, to taste

1 small shallot, minced

2 teaspoons white wine vinegar

3 tablespoons extra virgin olive oil

Endive Salad

Salade d'Endives

Belgian endive is at its best in winter, when its slightly bitter leaves are the most crisp and succulent. The sweet perfume of fresh pears, the saltiness of Roquefort and the richness of lightly toasted walnuts serve as contrasting but balanced flavors. Serve this as a first course at your next winter fête for a lovely flavorful beginning.

Cut the pears into ½-inch thick slices and toss them with the lemon juice in a small bowl. Rinse the endive and pat dry. Separate the leaves and fan them in a circle on a medium-sized platter. Make two layers if necessary, alternating with the pear slices. Crumble the Roquefort on top. Drizzle the dressing over the endive and pears. Sprinkle the toasted walnuts over the salad. Serve immediately.

If you would like, you can serve the endive on a bed of wild field greens.

Serves 4

Shallot Vinaigrette

In a small bowl mix the salt, pepper, shallot and vinegar. Slowly add the olive oil, whisking constantly, until thoroughly combined.

Serves 4

Pears add sweetness to the pleasantly bitter endive.

*Wild Field Greens
with Foie Gras*

sea salt, to taste

freshly ground black pepper, to taste

1 tablespoon balsamic vinegar

3 tablespoons extra virgin olive oil

10 cups wild field greens (Mesclun)

1 small, fresh foie gras (about 1 pound)
sliced into ½-inch thick pieces

2 tablespoons sherry vinegar

Wild Field Greens with Foie Gras

Mesclun au Foie Gras

In France, the year-end Holidays are not considered complete until foie gras is served at least once. It comes in many forms: in a terrine, cooked in salt, stuffed into a turkey, wrapped around truffles or fresh, as prepared here. All are delicious.

No matter the preparation, foie gras deserves light treatment. Here it is quickly sautéed in a very hot pan, then deglazed with sherry vinegar to balance its subtle and rich flavor. Set the foie gras atop fresh greens; it is, quite simply, divine.

To make the vinaigrette, place the salt, pepper and the balsamic vinegar in a large bowl and slowly whisk in the olive oil. Add the salad greens and toss until they are thoroughly coated. Evenly divide the salad greens among 6 salad plates.

Heat a non-stick skillet over medium high heat until it is hot. Add the slices of foie gras and cook, constantly gently shaking the pan, until browned on one side, about 1 minute. Turn and brown for 30 seconds on the other side, then add the sherry vinegar. Shake the pan so that the vinegar touches all the slices of foie gras and remove from the heat.

Transfer two slices of the foie gras to each salad, arranging them on top. Drizzle the foie gras with equal amounts of the cooking juices. Season lightly with salt and pepper, and serve immediately.

Serves 6

The secret to perfect foie gras is to sear quickly.

Les Notes

Les Plats de Résistance
Dinner Specialties

Shrimp and Lobster Pastis

Salmon and Seabass with Beurre Blanc Sauce

Beef en Croûte

Roasted Leg of Lamb Sauce Mirepoix

Duck à l'Orange

Roast Turkey

Chicken with Champagne

Shrimp and Lobster Pastis

2 tablespoons extra virgin olive oil

1 clove garlic, minced

2 medium tomatoes, diced

4 rock lobster tails

16 large shrimp, peeled and deveined
(32 if not using lobster tails)

3 tablespoons pastis

½ cup heavy cream

¼ stick unsalted butter

sea salt, to taste

ground black pepper, to taste

Shrimp and Lobster Pastis

Pastis de Crevettes et de Homard

Pastis is the drink of choice in Provence, where its anise flavor perfectly accompanies the region's lively cuisine. In this lovely and festive dish, pastis enhances the shellfish, lending an intriguing provençale lilt. This dish, which deserves to be served for a special occasion, is quick to prepare and makes for an impressive presentation.

Try this with fat Maine lobster tails or just with shrimp — either way it creates a fête all on its own!

Place the olive oil in a skillet over medium heat, add garlic and cook until the garlic turns translucent, approximately 4 minutes. Add the tomatoes, stir, then add the lobster tails and cook for an additional 4 minutes. Add the shrimp to the skillet and cook, stirring constantly for another 2 minutes.

Remove the skillet from the heat and add the pastis while shaking the skillet. Return the skillet to the heat, holding it carefully away from direct heat or flame as the pastis may catch fire. If the pastis ignites, it will quickly burn out.

Cook for about 3 minutes, constantly shaking the pan. Add the cream and cook, stirring frequently, until the liquid reduces by about one-third. Remove from the heat, stir in the butter, and season to taste with salt and pepper. Serve immediately.

Serves 4

Pernod and Ricard are popular brands of pastis.

*Salmon and Seabass
with Beurre Blanc Sauce*

4 tablespoons unsalted butter

4 tablespoons shallots, minced

1 cup dry white wine

¼ cup lemon juice

1 cup heavy cream

¼ cup olive oil

4 pieces salmon filets,
4 ounces each

4 pieces sea bass, 4 ounces each

1 teaspoon sea salt

½ teaspoon ground white pepper

Salmon and Seabass with Beurre Blanc Sauce

Saumon et Bar au Beurre Blanc

The elegance of salmon and the richness of sea bass combined with a classic French beurre blanc, make this dish fit for the finest occasion. Reserve this for New Year's Eve supper or save it for your favorite family celebration. Make the sauce before you cook the fish, and keep it warm in a hot water bath.

Place 1 tablespoon of the butter and the shallots in a medium saucepan and cook over medium heat, stirring frequently until the shallots are transparent, about 3 minutes.

Add the wine and lemon juice and bring to the boil. Boil until the liquid is reduced by half, about 5 minutes.

Add the cream, stir, and bring to a boil. Reduce the heat so the mixture simmers and cook until the sauce is slightly thickened, about 2 minutes.

Whisk in the remaining butter, working on and off the heat so the butter emulsifies but doesn't melt into the sauce. Season to taste with salt and pepper. Keep the sauce warm in a hot water bath.

Rinse the fish with cool water. Pat dry and refrigerate until just before cooking.

Heat the oil in a large skillet over medium heat until hot but not smoking. Add the filets; season them lightly in the skillet with the salt and pepper, and brown on one side, about 2 minutes. Turn the fish and season again with salt and pepper. Cover the pan. Cook until the fish is opaque through and golden, another 2 to 3 minutes.

Place the filets on a warmed platter. Let sit for about 3 minutes, and then drain any liquid given off by the fish. To serve, place one filet of each fish on a warmed dinner plate and cover with the sauce. Garnish each plate with flat-leaf parsley sprigs or with edible flowers such as geraniums or pansies.

Serve immediately.

Serves 4

You can also use halibut, snapper, tuna or swordfish.

Beef en Croûte

2 tablespoons extra virgin olive

2 pound beef tenderloin, trimmed

sea salt, to taste

ground black pepper, to taste

1 egg

1 pound Feuilletage Dough (page 86)
or use frozen puff pastry dough, thawed

2 cups Mushroom Duxelle
(page 49)

Beef en Croûte

Boeuf en Croûte

Golden pastry, tender beef and earthy mushrooms make Beef en Croûte a celebration all its own. Use the best quality beef you can find, and make sure the beef and mushrooms are completely cooled before wrapping them in the pastry.

Heat the oil in a medium sized pan large enough to hold the beef. When the oil is hot but not smoking, brown the beef on all sides, which should take about 5 minutes. Remove the tenderloin from the pan and season with salt and pepper. Let the beef cool to room temperature.

Whisk the egg with 1 teaspoon of water in a small bowl.

When the beef is cool, place puff pastry onto a lightly floured surface. The width of the dough should be about 1 inch wider than the tenderloin.

Brush the entire dough with egg wash. Spread the Mushroom Duxelles evenly across the bottom half of the dough.

Place the beef on top of the Mushroom Duxelles. Roll the dough around the tenderloin like a jellyroll, so that it is encased. The egg wash will act as a sealant, so the dough will stick together. Tuck the ends of the dough underneath the roll to enclose the tenderloin completely.

When fully rolled, brush the pastry with the remaining egg wash. Pierce the dough in several places to allow steam to escape during cooking.

Place the roll on a baking pan that has been lightly greased with butter. Bake in a preheated 400° oven until the pastry is well browned, approximately 20 minutes.

Remove from the oven and allow to rest for 15 minutes before slicing. The meat will be medium rare once the pastry is browned.

If you prefer, you can also make individual Beef en Croûte by slicing the tenderloin into equal portions and wrapping each slice in puff pastry.

Serves 4-6

Black Angus beef is ideal to use in this recipe.

*Roast Leg of Lamb
Sauce Mirepoix*

4-5 pound leg of lamb

2 tablespoons extra virgin olive oil

3 tablespoons sea salt

1 tablespoon cracked black pepper

2 large cloves fresh garlic

6 sprigs fresh rosemary

1 cup carrots, chopped

1 cup celery, chopped

1 cup yellow onions, chopped

1 cup water

½ cup dry red wine

Roasted Leg of Lamb Sauce Mirepoix

Gigot d'Agneau à la Mirepoix

Roast lamb creates its own celebration, particularly in France where it is a favorite dish. The best French lamb grazes on the salt marshes near Mont St. Michel, and it is indeed exceptional. However, French lamb is raised with such care throughout the country that it is difficult to go wrong no matter the region.

The French prefer lamb cooked rare, which they consider offers its best flavor and texture. If you prefer yours more well done, simply cook it as suggested below. Serve this succulent roast with Potato Gratin, and follow it with a crisp green salad.

Preheat the oven to 400°. Place the lamb in a large baking dish.

Rub the lamb with 1 tablespoon of oil. Season with salt and pepper.

Peel the garlic cloves and cut them vertically into 6 equal pieces. Make 12 slits in the meatiest parts of the lamb, and insert the pieces of garlic into the slits. Lay the rosemary sprigs atop the lamb.

In a small bowl combine the carrots, celery and onions. Toss the vegetables with the remaining olive oil, then scatter them around the lamb. Roast the lamb for 30 minutes, fatty side up. Turn the lamb and roast for an additional 30 minutes, then turn again and continue roasting until it reaches an internal temperature of 125° for rare lamb, about 10 more minutes to 145° for medium lamb, or about 20 additional minutes to 165° for well done lamb.

Remove the lamb from the oven and transfer to a cutting board. Sprinkle generously with salt and pepper, and let the lamb rest so the cooking juices retreat back into the meat before slicing.

While the lamb rests, make the sauce. Add the water and the wine to the roasting pan to deglaze, and bring to a boil over medium-high heat. Reduce heat to medium and cook, scraping the pan to remove any brown bits, until the liquid is reduced by half, about 10 minutes. Adjust the seasoning.

Slice the lamb into thin slices, and arrange on a warm serving platter. Strain the sauce over the lamb, pressing hard with a wooden spoon to extract all the juices. Garnish the platter with rosemary sprigs and serve.

Serves 6-8

Duck à l'Orange

Duck à l'Orange

1 whole duck, approximately 5 pounds, excess fat removed

6 tablespoons Holiday Seasoning (page 10)

sea salt, to taste

cracked black pepper, to taste

2 whole oranges

1 shallot, diced

¼ cup unsalted butter

1 cup orange juice

2 tablespoons Grand Marnier

1 tablespoon brown sugar

flat leaf parsley sprigs, to garnish

Canard à l'Orange

Duck à l'Orange is as classic to French cuisine as climbing the Eiffel Tower is to visiting Paris. Reserved for special holiday meals and fêtes, Duck à l'Orange never fails to impress with its golden skin and rich orange aroma. This recipe is a contemporary version of the classic, with its fennel and orange zest blend that is slipped under the skin so that the subtle aromas permeate the breast meat while the duck roasts. The sauce is a perfect complement with its buttery orange sweetness. Save this recipe for a very special occasion – you'll get rave reviews.

Preheat the oven to 450°.

Gently loosen the skin on the breast of the duck, and put all but 1 tablespoon of the holiday seasoning between the skin and the meat. Remove the giblets from the duck. Salt and pepper the cavity. Stuff the whole oranges inside the cavity, then add the giblets. Truss the duck and place in a roasting pan, breast side up. Roast the duck uncovered in the preheated oven for 30 minutes.

Turn the duck on its breast and roast for another 30 minutes, then turn it breast side up. Sprinkle the duck with the remaining holiday seasoning and continue roasting until the skin is golden brown and the juices run clear when the thigh is pierced with a skewer, an additional 10 to 15 minutes. Remove the duck from the oven and turn it on its breast and let rest for at least 15 minutes before serving.

Place the shallots and 1 tablespoon chilled butter in a small saucepan. Cook, stirring over medium heat until the shallots become translucent and begin to brown at the edges, about 5 minutes.

Add the orange juice, Grand Marnier and the brown sugar. Bring to a boil over medium high heat, and reduce the heat so the liquid gently boils and reduces by half.

Reduce the heat to low and simmer. Whisk the remaining cold butter into the liquid in small pieces, working on and off the heat, so that it emulsifies into the liquid. Be very careful not to boil the sauce.

Carve the duck and arrange it on a warmed serving platter. Serve the sauce next to the duck and garnish with parsley sprigs.

Serves 4

Be sure to add the butter to the sauce over very low heat.

Roast Turkey

1 fresh turkey, 14 pounds

sea salt

ground black pepper

2 lemons, halved

8 bay leaves

½ cup extra virgin olive oil

1 cup dry white wine or water

Roast Turkey

Dinde Rotie

About three weeks before Christmas, French farmers' markets become a turkey beauty pageant. The birds are brought live to market, squawking and wagging their heads, waiting to be chosen for someone's Christmas dinner. Prior to the market, the turkeys are coddled and fattened, resulting in succulent fowl whose meat has a rich and deep flavor. The French simply roast their birds as below, and serve them with roasted potatoes and a medley of vegetables.

Remove the neck and giblets from the turkey. Season the cavity with salt and pepper. Squeeze one of the halved lemons into the cavity. Put the squeezed and unsqueezed lemon halves into the turkey cavity.

Carefully slip your fingers between the skin and the meat on the breast and the legs of the turkey. Slip the bay leaves between the skin and the meat, arranging one in each leg, and three on each side of the breast in an attractive pattern. Rub the turkey all over with the olive oil and place in a roasting pan.

Create a tent of aluminum foil over the turkey.

Place the turkey into a preheated 350° oven. Cook for about 30 minutes per pound or until the internal temperature reaches 165°. Remove the foil from the turkey about an hour before it is finished, so the skin will turn golden brown. When the turkey is fully roasted the leg will move easily in the socket. Remove from the oven and carefully turn the turkey on its breast, so the juices run back into the meat. Let rest for at least 20 minutes before serving.

Add 1 cup dry white wine or water to the cooking juices in the pan and bring to a boil over medium-high heat. Simmer, stirring and scraping the bottom of the pan, until the liquid has reduced by about one-third. Season to taste and serve with the turkey.

Serves 8-10

Free range turkey will add extra flavor.

Chicken with Champagne
Poulet au Champagne

Nothing speaks of a fête more than Champagne, and here it delicately bathes chicken with its light floral bouquet. What's best about this recipe, aside from the juicy grapes and silken cream sauce, is the leftover Champagne which can be enjoyed before, during and after this lovely holiday dish.

Place the flour on a piece of waxed paper. Season with salt and several grinds of pepper and mix with your fingers. Dredge the chicken in the flour until well coated.

Heat the oil and butter in a large saucepan. Sauté the chicken over medium-high heat until browned on both sides, about 3 to 4 minutes per side.

Remove the chicken from the pan and drain any excess oil. Add the Champagne and the grapes to the pan, stir and cook for 5 minutes. Add the cream and parsley, then add the chicken breasts, turning them to coat with the liquid. Bring the liquid to a boil, reduce the heat to a simmer and cook, partially covered, until the chicken is cooked through, about 10 minutes. Garnish with additional parsley sprigs.

Serves 4

Chicken with Champagne

¼ cup all purpose flour

1 teaspoon sea salt

fresh ground black pepper, to taste

4 pieces boneless chicken breast

2 tablespoons unsalted butter

2 tablespoons canola oil

¾ cup Champagne

2 cups green grapes

¼ cup heavy cream

1 cup fresh parsley, minced and gently packed

For an Alsatian flavor, use Reisling instead of Champagne.

Les Notes

Les Notes

Les Legumes
Vegetables

Green Beans with Almonds and Tomatoes

Carrot and Butternut Squash Soufflé

Cranberry, Raspberry & Orange Relish

Mushroom Duxelle

Spinach with Cream

Chestnuts and Red Cabbage

Potato Gratin

Mashed Potatoes and Celery Root

la Madeleine Seven Grain Stuffing

1 pound haricots verts

¼ cup almonds, sliced

1 tablespoon extra virgin olive oil

1 tablespoon fresh garlic, minced

1 medium tomato, diced

1 teaspoon fresh thyme

sea salt, to taste

freshly ground pepper, to taste

Green Beans with Almonds and Tomatoes

Haricots Verts aux Amandes et à la Tomate

Haricots verts are thin French green beans that cook very quickly and are crisp and full of flavor. You can find these in any specialty market or substitute with the freshest green beans you can find.

In France, these are picked at the beginning of summer when their flavor is at the fullest. What is not eaten is then canned and saved for winter feasts.

Clean the green beans by removing the stems at each end. Blanch green beans in boiling salt water until they turn bright green, about 20 seconds. Plunge immediately into a bowl of ice water.

Sauté the almonds in a pan over medium heat until toasted to a golden hue, about 3 minutes.

Put the olive oil and the garlic into a sauté pan and place over medium heat.

When the garlic begins to turn golden add the green beans and sauté for 5 minutes or until tender.

When the beans are just about cooked, add tomatoes and cook until hot, stirring constantly. Remove from the heat; add the almonds, then add the thyme. Season with salt and pepper and serve immediately.

Serves 4

If you use American green beans, cook a little longer.

*Carrot and Butternut
Squash Soufflé*

2 medium carrots,
peeled and diced

1 small (10 ounce) butternut squash,
peeled, seeded and cubed

½ cup heavy cream

2 whole eggs

sea salt, to taste

pinch of white pepper

¼ teaspoon ground nutmeg

Carrot and Butternut Squash Soufflé

Soufflé de Carotte et de Courgette

This delicate, bright orange soufflé is not only gorgeous to look at but also tastes luscious with its intriguing carrot, squash and nutmeg flavor combination. It celebrates none other than the best that Autumn has to offer and is an ideal side dish to Roast Turkey – a favorite Holiday dish.

This recipe can be easily doubled. If you do so, you'll want to slightly increase the baking time, watching carefully at the end of cooking to prevent burning. You can also prepare this dish in six individual ramekins by filling each about two-thirds full and baking for 15 minutes.

Cover the carrots with water and cook over medium heat for 5 minutes. Add the butternut squash and cook until the carrots and squash are tender.

Drain and puree the vegetables using a handheld mixer or a food processor. Transfer to a medium-sized bowl and whisk in the cream, eggs, salt, pepper and nutmeg.

Pour the vegetable mixture into a buttered 6-inch souffle mold and bake in a preheated 375° oven for 25 minutes or until the soufflé splits slightly on top and is set.

Serve immediately.

Serves 4

Grate your own nutmeg and taste the difference!

Cranberry, Raspberry & Orange Relish

Coulis de Canneberges, Framboises et Orange

Cranberries have a wonderfully vivid flavor. Now imported into France, they are fast becoming a French favorite. This relish, with its flavor and gorgeous red color, makes any table festive, and it is the ideal accompaniment to a Holiday Roast Turkey. Don't miss its starring role as a seasoning on a post Holiday turkey sandwich.

In a saucepan, combine all of the ingredients except the cornstarch. Simmer until the cranberries split open and are very soft.

In a separate bowl mix the cornstarch with ⅛ cup water to form a liquid paste.

Slowly add the cornstarch to the cranberries and simmer over low heat, until the relish starts to thicken.

Stir well and let chill in the refrigerator until serving time.

Makes 3 cups

Mushroom Duxelle

Duxelle de Champignons

Mushroom Duxelle make a wonderful and very traditional filling for Beef en Croûte. Mushroom Duxelle also makes a delicious side dish. For a special treat, add foie gras and serve with roast game or an equally special celebratory dish.

Melt the butter in a skillet over medium heat. When the butter foams, add the onion and garlic and sauté until translucent, about 6 minutes. Add the mushrooms, red wine and bay leaves increase the heat to medium-high.

Cook slowly, stirring occasionally until all the liquid is evaporated, about 15 minutes. Remove the bay leaf and discard.

Season with salt and pepper.

Makes 2 cups

Cranberry, Raspberry & Orange Relish

2 cups granulated sugar

24 ounces fresh cranberries

1 cup fresh raspberries

2 teaspoons orange zest

2 cups orange juice

¼ cup Grand Marnier

½ cup cornstarch

Mushroom Duxelle

2 tablespoons unsalted butter

1 medium yellow onion, diced

1 tablespoon fresh garlic, minced

1 pound button mushrooms, cleaned and sliced

1 cup dry red wine

3 bay leaves

½ teaspoon cracked black pepper

sea salt, to taste

Spinach with Cream

2 pounds fresh spinach,
cleaned and stemmed

¾ cup heavy cream

⅛ teaspoon nutmeg

sea salt, to taste

cracked black pepper, to taste

Chestnuts and Red Cabbage

2 cups chestnuts, fresh or whole bottled
chestnuts

1 small (1 ½ pounds) red cabbage

¼ cup brown sugar

¾ cup white wine vinegar

⅓ cup golden raisins

1 quart chicken stock

cracked black pepper, to taste

1 teaspoon sea salt

Spinach with Cream
Épinards à la Crème

Everyone, even the most anti-spinach of us all, loves spinach with cream. Perhaps it is the way it melts into the fresh cream or the sweet spark of nutmeg. Whatever it may be, this is an ideal accompaniment to any Holiday meal.

Steam the spinach until limp. Place in a tea towel and squeeze most of the water out, so that it is slightly moist, but not wet.

Warm the spinach in a sauce pan over medium heat. Stir in the cream and add the nutmeg. Cook until the spinach and cream thicken. Stir in the remaining cream and heat until the mixture is hot.

Season to taste with salt and pepper and serve.

Serves 4-6

Chestnuts and Red Cabbage
Châtaignes et Chou Rouge

In the fall, children help gather chestnuts, finding humor in avoiding jabs from the prickly chestnut casing. This dish, which hails from eastern France, is not only gorgeous, with its purple cabbage and toasty-brown chestnuts, but also delicious.

Serve it as an ideal accompaniment to a Holiday Roast Turkey or Beef en Croûte. You'll be delighted at the color – and flavor – it adds to your meal.

If you are using fresh chestnuts, place chestnuts into a large pot and cover with water. Bring to a boil, and immediately reduce heat to simmer for 25 minutes. Strain and place chestnuts onto a baking pan. Bake in a preheated 350° oven for 45 minutes or until the chestnuts split open. Cool, then remove from the shell and reserve.

In a large saucepan, add all the ingredients except the chestnuts. Mix well and bring to a boil over medium heat. Reduce the heat to a simmer and cover. Simmer for 45 minutes or until cabbage is very tender. Remove the lid and add the chestnuts.

Cook, uncovered, until half of the cooking juices have evaporated and the chestnuts are hot and tender, about 15 to 20 minutes. Season to taste with salt and pepper.

Serves 8-10

Potato Gratin

2 cups heavy cream

1 cup half-and-half

1 clove garlic, minced

2 teaspoons sea salt

ground black pepper, to taste

2 ¼ pounds sliced red potatoes,
sliced ⅛-inch thick

1 ½ cups Gruyère, grated

Potato Gratin

Pommes de Terre au Gratin

Nothing speaks more of sumptuous home cooking than a rich creamy potato gratin, and this one is exceptional. Serve it alongside a Holiday Roast Turkey or Beef en Croûte for a traditional and elegant meal. Remember to make this in a pretty dish that can go straight from the oven to the table. We think you'll find this will become a family favorite and a Holiday meal tradition.

Combine the cream, half-and-half, garlic, salt and pepper in a large saucepan. Add the sliced potatoes and stir well to completely coat them with the cream mixture. Bring to a simmer and cook for 25 minutes or until the potatoes are tender. Stir occasionally. Do not let the potatoes boil.

When potatoes are tender, adjust the seasonings and pour into a 8x10-inch baking dish. Sprinkle with the cheese and bake in the center of a preheated 425° oven until golden on top and the potatoes are completely tender, about 20 minutes.

Serves 8

Add cooked bacon or ham for a hearty lunch dish.

Mashed Potatoes and Celery Root

1 pound celery root,
peeled and cut into 1-inch dice

2 pounds Yukon Gold potatoes,
peeled and quartered

½ cup milk

¼ cup unsalted butter

2 teaspoons sea salt

1 teaspoon ground black pepper

Mashed Potatoes and Celery Root

Purée de Pommes de Terre et Céleri Rave

Fabulous mashed potatoes are as traditionally French as the Marseillaise, and equally as well loved. This recipe, a heavenly combination of potatoes and celery root, softened with milk and butter is ideal for a memorable meal. This is the perfect accompaniment to Duck à l'Orange, Roast Turkey or Salmon and Sea Bass with Beurre Blanc. Light and flavorful, they are best eaten immediately after preparation.

Put celery root and potatoes in a large saucepan and cover with water. Bring to a boil and cook until the vegetables are very tender. Drain.

While the potatoes and celery root cook, simmer the milk and butter in a small saucepan.

Place potatoes and the celery root in a large serving bowl and whip with the whisk attachment of an electric mixer until the desired consistency.

Add the warm milk and butter mixture and continue to whip until the vegetables are light and fluffy.

Season to taste with salt and pepper. Serve immediately.

Serves 6

Yukon Gold potatoes add a special "je ne sais quoi".

La Madeleine Seven Grain Stuffing

Farce aux Sept Graines à la Madeleine

Stuffing is a very personal thing. There are those who want only sage flavors, others who insist on mushrooms, others who won't even consider it if it contains onions. This stuffing, a French-influenced version of an American classic, is likely to please everyone. Intended to be baked on its own, it can also be used to stuff a turkey, chicken, duck or goose. But don't wait for your favorite poultry or special occasion to make this delicious stuffing. Create a celebration and serve this all on its own – it's delicious!

Preheat oven to 350˚.

Place all but 1 tablespoon of the butter into a skillet. Add the onions, garlic, apples and celery and cook over medium heat, stirring until the onions turn translucent, about 5 minutes.

Add the mushrooms and bacon and simmer until the mushrooms have released some of their liquid and the bacon is cooked, 3 to 4 minutes.

Add the bread, stir, and add the chicken broth, oregano and a light seasoning of salt and pepper.

With the remaining tablespoon of butter, coat a medium sized baking pan, and place the stuffing in it. Cover with aluminum foil and bake until the stuffing is soft, about 35 minutes.

Remove the foil and continue baking until the stuffing is crisp and golden on top, an additional 10 minutes. Remove from the oven and serve.

Serves 8

La Madeleine Seven Grain Stuffing

1 stick unsalted butter

1 medium onion, diced

2 cloves garlic, minced

¼ cup red apples, diced

⅛ cup celery, diced

½ pound button mushrooms, thinly sliced

¼ raw bacon, diced

1 pound day old seven grain bread, cut into 1-inch cubes

3 cups chicken broth

2 tablespoons dried oregano

sea salt, to taste.

ground black pepper, to taste

Apples add sweetness to this stuffing.

Les Notes

Les Notes

Les Desserts et les Pains

Desserts & Breads

Holiday Cookies

Petits Gateaux de Fête

This traditional French dough is the basis for many delicious cookies, including la Madeleine's signature Linzer Cookies. French families prepare batches of these cookies in a variety of shapes and sizes in November, and serve them with coffee and tea throughout the Holidays.

½ stick unsalted butter, softened

¾ cup granulated sugar

2 eggs

½ teaspoon salt

zest of one lemon

1 teaspoon natural vanilla extract

2 cups all purpose flour

1 tablespoon baking powder

pinch of ground cloves

½ teaspoon ground cinnamon

½ cup almonds, ground

¼ cup hazelnuts, ground

1 egg, beaten

Using an electric mixer, combine the butter, sugar, egg, salt, lemon zest and vanilla until blended. Mix in the flour along with the baking powder, cloves, cinnamon, almonds and hazelnuts.

Do not overmix the dough; stop when the dough is well combined. Wrap the dough in plastic wrap, and chill at least 2 hours, or preferably overnight, before using.

Roll the dough out on a lightly floured surface and cut the cookies into your favorite shapes.

Place the cookies on a greased baking pan or a pan lined with parchment paper. Brush the cookies with the beaten egg.

Bake in preheated 350° oven for 12 to 15 minutes.

Cookies can be brushed with a mixture of confectioner's sugar and rum. This must be done when the cookies are still hot so the alcohol will evaporate. Simply pour rum over confectioner's sugar and mix to form a thin, brushable paste.

Makes 36 cookies

The less you mix the dough, the crisper the cookie.

Linzer Cookies

**Holiday Cookie Dough
(page 60)**

One jar seedless raspberry jam

½ cup confectioners' sugar

Linzer Cookies

Les Tartelettes Linzer

These delicate little tiered cookies with raspberry filling are favorites at la Madeleine. Nutty and seductively spiced, they are an updated version of a traditional Lunette cookie, and typical of the many Holiday cookies made in the Alsace region in eastern France. Lovely and buttery tasting, they look beautiful with their shiny red filling and snowy white décor.

On a well-floured surface, roll out the cookie dough to approximately ³⁄₁₆-inch thick, working quickly.

Cut out the cookies using a 2-inch round scalloped cookie cutter.

Reform the dough, and cut out more cookies until no cookie dough is left. Be careful not to overmix the dough when reforming it; simply stack the individual pieces and reroll the dough.

Place the cookies on a baking pan lined with parchment paper, ½ inch apart. Cut out the centers of half of the cookies using a ¾- to 1-inch round cookie cutter.

Bake the cookies in a preheated 325° oven for 15 minutes or until golden brown.

Set aside to cool.

Spread ½ teaspoon of seedless raspberry jam on each bottom cookie. Sprinkle the "cut-out" cookies with the confectioners' sugar to form the top tier of the cookie, and place together.

If the cookie needs more jam in the center, simply pipe or spoon more jam into the center cutout.

Makes 18 cookies

Sprinkle the tops with colored sugar for holiday flair.

Almond Tuiles

Tuiles aux Amandes

Tuiles are a classic petit four, presented after a sumptuous feast along with coffee, to be savored as the evening winds down. Every baker has his own recipe for these crisp lace cookies and these, developed by Chef Remy Schaal, are head and shoulders above them all. Nutty and golden tasting they benefit from the addition of browned butter, a little trick that adds a lovely flavor dimension.

Make only 6 Tuiles at a time. They cool so quickly, if you make more they will become too crisp to handle. Transfer them immediately from the baking sheet to a wooden broom handle or rolling pin to give them their characteristic roof tile shape.

Mix the almonds, sugar and flour in a mixing bowl using a wooden spoon. Add the egg whites and vanilla and mix well. Make the buerre noisette and while still hot, mix into the ingredients immediately.

Let the batter rest in the refrigerator overnight.

Place heaping teaspoon-sized dollops of the batter on a well-greased cookie sheet.

Use the back of a fork dipped in cold water to flatten each dollop as thin as possible forming an approximately 2- to 2 ½-inch round cookie. Bake in a preheated 325˚ oven for 12 minutes, or until golden around the edges.

Remove from the oven and immediately remove the tuiles from the baking pan with a metal spatula. Working quickly, place each Tuile on a rolling pin or a wooden broomstick handle laid across the backs of two chairs. Gently bend them around the rolling pin or broom handle to give them their curved French roof tile shape.

Serve as soon as they are crisp, or store them in a tightly sealed container, as they are most delicious when very fresh and crisp.

Makes about 40 Tuiles

Beurre Noisette

In a heavy saucepan, on medium heat, melt the ½ stick of butter until it turns a light caramel color, about 4 minutes. Be careful not to burn the butter.

The key to success with tuiles is to work quickly.

Almond Tuile Cookies

½ cup almonds, sliced

1 cup granulated sugar

¾ cup all purpose flour

6 egg whites

1 teaspoon natural
vanilla extract

Beurre Noisette

½ stick butter

Pain d'Épices

2 ½ cups all purpose flour

½ teaspoon salt

2 teaspoons baking soda

½ teaspoon baking powder

1 teaspoon cinnamon

2 teaspoons spice blend

⅓ cup honey

½ cup granulated sugar

1 egg yolk

½ cup milk

Spice Blend

¾ teaspoon cloves, ground

¾ teaspoon aniseeds, ground

⅜ teaspoon nutmeg, ground

⅜ teaspoon ginger, ground

Royal Icing

2 egg whites

1 cup confectioners' sugar

Pain d'Épices

Pain d'Épices

The entire region of Alsace lights up for the Holidays, perhaps more than any other region in France. Homes and businesses are decorated, and special markets are held where the air is fragrant with the aroma of spicy Pain d'Épices. These cookies are cut into fanciful shapes and given as gifts.

In a mixing bowl, combine the flour, salt, baking soda, baking powder, cinnamon and spices. Start mixing at low speed with an electric mixer. Add the honey, sugar and egg yolk. Continue mixing at low speed.

As the dough forms, carefully start adding the milk. You may not need to add all of the milk; start with ¼ of a cup and slowly add more milk until the dough becomes firm but sticky.

When the dough is well combined, wrap the dough in plastic wrap and refrigerate for 24 hours.

On a lightly floured surface, roll out the dough to ³⁄₁₆-inch thickness.

Cut out the cookies with your choice of cookie cutters and place them ½ inch apart on a well-greased baking pan.

Bake in a preheated oven at 325° for 10 to 12 minutes or until the edges of the cookies just start to turn brown. Let them cool on the pan for 5 minutes, and then remove to a cooling rack.

For decoration, soft royal icing can be brushed over each cookie. Let dry at room temperature for 24 hours before storing.

Makes 2 dozen cookies

Spice Blend

Mix all the ingredients until well blended.

Royal Icing

Whip two egg whites with ¾ cup of the confectioners' sugar for 2 minutes. Continue to add confectioners' sugar until the icing forms a brushable paste. Cover the top of the bowl with a wet cloth to prevent the icing from drying out.

Stollen

Stollen

This is Chef Remy Schaal's version of Stollen, a traditional German sweet loaf that is also common in Alsace. It has a characteristic light French touch, with a lovely tender crumb and delicate spicing. It also has a very American touch, with the addition of pecans, the only nut indigenous to the United States. One secret to excellent stollen is top-quality candied fruit, so use the best you can find.

Pour the rum over the raisins and candied fruit, let it sit overnight.

In an electric mixer fitted with the dough hook attachment, combine the flour, sugar, salt, spices and yeast. Add the milk and eggs and mix at low speed. Add the butter and mix for 10 minutes, until the dough is smooth and forms a ball.

Add the candied fruit mixture and the pecans and mix only until well combined. Set the dough aside and let it rise at room temperature for 3 hours or until the dough doubles in volume.

Divide the dough into two parts and form each part into a ball. Shape each ball into a loaf and flatten half the loaf lengthwise with a rolling pin. As you would with a turnover, return the flattened part of the loaf onto the top of the loaf.

Place both loaves on a baking pan, and let them proof for 2-3 hours until doubled in volume.

Mix the granulated sugar with the cinnamon and reserve.

Place in a preheated 375° oven for 35 minutes, or until golden brown. Remove from the oven. Immediately brush with the melted butter and roll each loaf into the cinnamon sugar mixture. Set aside to cool.

Sprinkle the top of each loaf with confectioners' sugar and serve.

Makes 2 loaves

Stollen

2 tablespoons rum

1 cup raisins

⅓ cup candied oranges, diced

⅓ cup candied lemons, diced

½ cup candied cherries, diced

5 cups bread flour

½ cup granulated sugar

1 teaspoon salt

1 teaspoon cinnamon

½ teaspoon ground nutmeg

½ teaspoon ground allspice

1 packet granulated yeast

1 ½ cups milk

2 eggs

2 sticks butter, softened

¾ cup pecan pieces

4 tablespoons butter, melted

Cinnamon Sugar

⅓ cup granulated sugar

¼ teaspoon cinnamon

confectioners' sugar

Stollen will stay fresh for three weeks in an airtight container.

Mixed Berry Tart

½ cup granulated sugar

2 cups milk

3 tablespoons cornstarch

4 egg yolks

½ stick unsalted butter

1 teaspoon natural vanilla extract

9-inch prebaked Almond Tart shell
(page 81)

1 pint fresh blueberries

1 pint fresh raspberries

1 cup red currant jelly

Mixed Berry Tart

Tarte aux Trois Baies

This berry tart is a la Madeleine specialty. The crisp nutty pastry, smooth cream and seasonal fruit make this dessert a spectacular finalé for your Holiday festivities. Decorating with colorful fruit during the holidays is a French country tradition, so feel free to use any fruit or berry that you desire. Be sure to serve immediately after preparing, when this tart is at its best.

In a saucepan, add ¼ cup sugar to the milk and bring to a boil while stirring occasionally.

In a separate mixing bowl, combine the remaining sugar and the corn starch, add the egg yolks. Mix well with a whisk.

Once the milk is boiling, pour one fourth of the milk into the egg mixture to temper, stirring constantly. Pour the egg mixture into the rest of the milk and return to the heat, stirring until the cream thickens and comes to a complete boil.

Remove from the heat, add the butter and the vanilla, and stir until the butter completely melts. Pour the cream into a shallow bowl, cover with plastic wrap and let cool to room temperature. If not using immediately, store in an airtight container in the refrigerator.

Spread the cold pastry cream into the bottom of the tart shell, and cover with the fresh berries, arranged in concentric circles.

Melt the red currant jelly over medium heat. When liquified, carefully brush over the fruit using a pastry brush. Serve immediately.

Serves 8

You can be berry creative with your fruit selections!

Lavender Honey
Crème Brûlée

½ cup whipping cream

1 cup milk

1 cup granulated sugar

One whole vanilla bean
cut lengthwise

8 egg yolks

3 tablespoons lavender honey

6 teaspoons brown sugar

Lavender Honey Crème Brûlée

Crème Brûlée au Miele de Lavande

Crème brûlée is a creamy, egg-rich hallmark of French cuisine. The lavender honey, which lends a subtle perfume, makes this a true celebratory dessert, fit for linens, silver, candles and champagne.

Chill this dessert all the way through before caramelizing the sugar, to provide a lovely temperature contrast between the cold crème and the hot caramelized sugar.

Place the cream, milk and half the sugar in a medium-sized saucepan. Scrape the seeds from the vanilla bean into the milk mixture, then add the bean as well. Scald over medium heat. Remove from the heat, cover, and let infuse for 10 to 15 minutes.

In a separate bowl, blend the egg yolks with the remaining sugar. Remove the vanilla bean from the milk mixture and discard. Whisk the hot milk mixture into the eggs and sugar and then strain through a fine-mesh sieve. Whisk in the honey until thoroughly combined.

Place 6 ramekins into a baking pan and add water to the pan until it reaches half way up the sides of the ramekins. Divide the Crème Brulee mixture among the ramekins, cover the entire pan with aluminum foil and bake in a preheated 275° oven until the custards are set, about 50 minutes. Remove from the oven and the water bath. Let cool to room temperature, then refrigerate until cold, about 3 hours.

Before serving, preheat the broiler. Sprinkle 1 teaspoon brown sugar over each ramekin and place them 3 inches from the broiler until the sugar is evenly caramelized. Serve immediately.

Makes 6 servings

Use your favorite honey for this creamy dessert.

Chocolate Charlotte
Charlotte au Chocolat

Chef Remy Schaal remembers this dessert as one of his mother's favorites. She claimed it was easy to prepare, yet made for a dramatic presentation that was sure to please family and friends of all ages. She would sometimes make two versions; one with cognac for the adults and one without for the children.

In a saucepan, combine the sugar and water and bring to a boil over high heat. Remove from heat and chill. Once cold, add the 1 ½ teaspoons cognac.

Lightly brush each ladyfinger with the cognac syrup and immediately line a 6 cup charlotte mold or soufflé dish along the sides, rounded sides out. Trim the remaining ladyfingers to make a triangle and place them, pointed end toward the center, on the bottom of the mold until it is completely covered.

In a double boiler, melt the chocolate and the butter. Remove from the heat and let cool to room temperature. Whisk in the egg yolks and half of the sugar.

Whisk in 1 tablespoon of cognac.

Whip the cream to stiff peaks and fold into the chocolate mixture. Beat the egg white with the pinch of salt and the remaining sugar to a soft peak and fold into the chocolate and cream mixture.

Immediately pour into the ladyfinger-lined bowl and refrigerate until very cold, at least 4 hours.

Serves 6

Cognac Syrup

¼ cup granulated sugar

¼ cup water

1 ½ teaspoons cognac

Chocolate Charlotte

15 ladyfingers

8 ounces semi- sweet chocolate

1 stick unsalted butter

2 eggs, separated

1 cup granulated sugar

1 tablespoon cognac

2 cups whipping cream

pinch of salt

Use the best quality chocolate you can find.

Chocolate Darioles

4 ounces semi-sweet chocolate

1 stick unsalted butter, softened

Butter for the ramekins

5 whole eggs

½ cup granulated sugar

7 tablespoons all purpose flour

Whipped cream for garnish

Fresh raspberries for garnish

Chocolate Darioles

Darioles au Chocolat

These intense chocolate cakes, with a melted chocolate sauce inside, surprise and delight everyone. Easy and quick to make, they are the perfect finalé for an elegant Holiday meal. Bring them to the table garnished with cream and raspberries, and everyone will clamor for more.

Cut the chocolate into small pieces and begin melting in a double boiler. Stir occasionally using a wooden spoon.

Once the chocolate is melted, add the softened butter, stir and set aside. In a separate mixing bowl, whisk the eggs and sugar until light and fluffy. Carefully fold in the flour. Add the chocolate mixture and refrigerate for 2 hours.

Butter four 3 ½-inch ramekins and fill each with a generous ⅓ cup of the batter.

Bake in a preheated 375° oven for 8 to 10 minutes. The outside of the darioles should be cooked, but the inside should be liquid. Test with a cake tester.

Unmold the darioles immediately onto a serving plate. Garnish with whipped cream and raspberries.

Serve hot.

Serves 4

Don't overbake, you'll enjoy the soft center.

Tarte Tatin

¼ cup water

1 ½ cups granulated sugar

Four medium sized
Granny Smith apples

3 tablespoons unsalted butter

½ recipe Almond Tart Dough
(see page 81)

Crème Anglaise (page 78)

Tarte Tatin

Tarte Tatin

Tarte Tatin would win any French poll to determine the country's favorite dessert. Though it originated in the Loire Valley, it is common throughout France, where each baker adds his or her own special touch. Traditionally, Tarte Tatin is made and served when good cooking apples first ripen in September, and throughout the apple season in the winter; Tarte Tatin creates a festive occasion any time it is served. This recipe calls for Granny Smith apples, but any good, tart cooking apple will do. Serve with Crème Anglaise or with a dollop of freshly whipped cream.

Oil a 9-inch diameter non-stick cake pan and set aside.

Prepare a caramel by combining the water and ¾ cup sugar. Cook over medium-high heat, swirling occasionally, until the caramel turns a medium-brown color. Do not stir. Remove from the heat, and immediately pour into the bottom of the cake pan, spreading evenly.

Be careful when making the caramel as it is extremely hot (280°) and can cause serious burns.

Peel and core the apples, and cut each apple into 8 wedges. Line them on top of the caramel in a circular shape, keeping the apples upright.

Sprinkle the remaining granulated sugar over the top of the apples and spread small pieces of butter evenly across the top.

Roll out the Almond Tart Dough and cut out a circle the size of the top of the cake pan. Cover the apples with the dough. Bake in a preheated 325° oven until golden brown, about 50 minutes.

Let cool for 1 hour at room temperature. Place a serving dish on top of the baking pan and flip so that the Tarte Tatin is ready to be served. The dough will be on the bottom and the apples will be on the top. Serve with Crème Anglaise (page 78) or vanilla ice cream.

Serves 6

Bake this tarte slowly so the caramel coats the apples evenly.

Crème Anglaise

1 ½ cups milk

1 ½ cups heavy cream

1 cup granulated sugar

Half of a vanilla bean

5 egg yolks

Crème Anglaise

In a saucepan, combine the milk, cream and ⅓ cup sugar. Heat over medium heat.

Cut the vanilla bean lengthwise and scrape the soft inside into the liquid using the tip of a knife. Add the emptied vanilla bean to the mixture and scald over medium heat. Remove from the heat, cover and let stand for 10 minutes.

In a separate bowl, combine the egg yolks and the remaining sugar and immediately start whipping with a whisk. As the mixture turns a pale yellow add ¼ of the hot milk combination and mix. Add the egg and milk mixture to the remaining hot milk and whisk together until combined. Place on medium-low heat and whisk in a figure eight motion until thickened. Do not boil.

Immediately pour the crème into a cold bowl and continue to stir for a few moments to help cool. Chill in the refrigerator prior to serving.

Makes 3 cups

Be very careful not to boil the milk.

Roasted Apples
Pommes au Four

In France, roasted apples celebrate the advent of winter and months of cozy evenings around the fire perhaps more poignantly than anything else. As they bake, their stuffing fills the air with a spicy aroma, softened by the fragrance of the caramelizing sugar and the butter. The honey, sugar, butter, berries and citrus zest are a French influence – the walnuts, raisins and spices, American. Together they represent a luscious union. Serve Roasted Apples hot from the oven for dessert, or for an afternoon snack.

You may substitute red currants or blueberries for the gooseberries in this recipe. If you use frozen berries, do not thaw before mixing into the stuffing.

Preheat oven to 400°. Peel the top of the apple and remove the core, making a hole 1 ½ inch in diameter. Be sure to leave the base of the apple intact so that the filling does not leak out.

Mix all the filling ingredients together except for the butter and sugar. Fill each apple with equal amounts of filling, pressing it firmly inside the apple and mounding it slightly on top.

Place the apples close together in a shallow baking pan. Cut the butter into six equal pieces and top each apple with a piece of butter. Sprinkle equal amounts of the sugar over each apple.

Bake for 35 minutes, or until the apples are tender but not falling apart. Check them occasionally near the end of baking, and if the filling is too dark, cover the apples loosely with aluminum foil. Serve with vanilla ice cream or Darjeeling tea sauce.

Serves 6

Darjeeling Tea Sauce

Bring water and sugar to a boil. Add the tea bags and let cool to room temperature. Remove the tea bags and add the heavy cream.

Makes 1 ½ cups

Roasted Apples

6 Golden Delicious apples

1 cup gooseberries

¾ cup walnut pieces

zest of one lemon

zest of one orange

¾ cup raisins

¾ cup honey

pinch of allspice

pinch of ginger

pinch of cinnamon

6 tablespoons unsalted butter

¾ cup granulated sugar

Darjeeling Tea Sauce

⅔ cup water

⅔ cup granulated sugar

3 teabags Darjeeling tea

½ cup heavy cream

Génoise Roll

4 large eggs

⅔ cup granulated sugar

1 teaspoon natural vanilla extract

1 cup all purpose flour

Butter Cream

5 egg yolks

¾ cup powdered sugar

1 ½ sticks unsalted butter, softened

¼ cup toasted walnuts, ground

1 teaspoon natural vanilla extract

Christmas Log
Bûche de Noël

The Holidays wouldn't be the same without a Bûche de Noël. The log is usually purchased at the neighborhood bakery on Christmas Eve, to be eaten after a supper following midnight Mass. The renowned Lenôtre Bakery in Paris makes over twenty-five varieties of these Yule Logs, here is the la Madeleine version.

Why a log shape? In the Middle Ages, a fire in the hearth was a luxury. Guests would bring a wooden log as a holiday gift to their friends. Today, this traditional gift is replaced by a tastier tradition – a Bûche de Noël.

Génoise Roll

Lightly butter a 10x17-inch baking pan and then line with parchment paper. In an electric mixer fitted with the whip attachment, combine the eggs and sugar. Mix at high speed, until light, fluffy and pale yellow, about 5 minutes.

Remove the bowl from the mixer, whisk in the vanilla, and then slowly fold in the sifted flour. Fold only until combined.

Pour the mixture in the baking pan and spread out evenly to cover the entire surface. Bake immediately, in a preheated 400° oven for 10 minutes, or until a light golden color. Remove from the oven and place a damp tea towel over the entire surface to keep the cake moist. Set aside for later use.

Butter Cream

In an electric mixer fitted with the whip attachment, combine the egg yolks and sugar. Mix at high speed until light and fluffy. Drop the speed to low and add the softened butter, piece by piece, until well combined.

Toast the walnuts in a preheated 325° oven until golden brown, and let the walnuts cool to room temerature. Grind the walnuts and add with the vanilla to the butter mixture. Set aside. Whisk before using to make sure all the ingredients are thoroughly combined.

Assemble only after each part is finished.

Kirsch Syrup

¼ cup granulated sugar

¼ cup water

1 tablespoon Kirsch

Chocolate Ganache

½ cup whipping cream

12 ounces semi-sweet chocolate, chopped into small pieces

Kirsch Syrup

In a saucepan, combine the sugar and water, and bring to a boil. Remove from the heat and let cool to room temperature. Add the Kirsch and mix. Set aside for later use.

Chocolate Ganache

Pour the cream into a saucepan and bring to a boil, stirring occasionally. Remove from the heat. Add the chocolate pieces to the cream and let it sit until the chocolate is melted, swirling the pan occasionally. Using a wooden spoon, stir until well blended. Set aside to thicken at room temperature.

Assembly

Remove the parchment paper from the Génoise roll, trim the edges, and set the trimmings aside. Using a pastry brush, spread the kirsch syrup on top of the cake. Let the syrup soak in for a minute or two.

Spread the butter cream evenly over the entire surface of the Génoise roll and sprinkle with the raspberries.

Carefully roll up the filled cake (use the tea towel to help you roll the cake) to form a nice, round "log". Coat the exterior with the thickened Ganache. The tree bark effect can be achieved by pulling a fork the length of the frosting. Use the cake trimmings to form a knot.

You can decorate your Bûche de Noël with sugared fruits, meringue mushrooms, chocolate holly leaves, cranberries or raspberries.

Refrigerate for a least 1 hour before serving.

Makes 1 log, serves 8

Decorate with meringue mushrooms and chocolate holly leaves.

King's Cake

King's Cake is the highlight of winter in France. It is made to celebrate the feast of the Epiphany, in early January, when families gather around the table to "tirer la fève" in other words , to find the bean. This charm or bean is baked inside the Galette. Whoever finds the charm in their piece of King's Cake is crowned King for the Day, complete with a gold paper crown.

King's Cake is easy to make, and impressive to serve. In the old days, the charm was simply a dried bean. Today, however, charms might be anything from tiny ceramic cartoon figures to stars on the country's football team. Use whatever you like and do as most French do: arrange it so the youngest person at the table finds the charm.

Using an electric mixer fitted with the whip attachment mix the butter and sugar at high speed until light and fluffy. Add the egg and mix well. In a separate bowl, combine the almond meal and flour, and add to the egg mixture.

Add the rum and vanilla, and mix well.

On a lightly floured surface, roll out the puff pastry to ⅛-inch thickness. Cut out two 9-inch circles. Place them on a flat tray, and let the circles rest in the refrigerator for 1 hour. Take one of the pastry circles and brush egg wash around the edge, making a 1-inch wide border.

Spread the almond cream from the center out, leaving the 1 inch border free of cream. This is an important step since any almond cream left on the border may cause the cake to open during baking.

Put the charm in the almond cream and cover with the second layer of puff pastry. Press softly around the edges to seal the cream inside.

Brush the remaining egg wash on the top. Cut decorative shapes into the top of the pastry with the tip of a knife, careful not to puncture through the surface. Let the finished cake rest for 1 hour prior to baking.

Bake in a preheated 400° oven for 45 minutes, or until the cake is golden brown. If the cake starts to brown too quickly, cover loosely with aluminum foil so it continues to bake but does not brown.

Remove from the oven and cool on a wire rack for 10 minutes before serving.

Serves 8

King's Cake

1 stick unsalted butter, softened

½ cup granulated sugar

1 egg

½ cup almond meal (see page 81)

¼ cup all purpose flour

1 tablespoon rum, optional

1 teaspoon natural vanilla extract

1 ½ pounds Feuilletage Dough
(see page 86) or frozen puff pastry
dough, thawed

1 feve or charm

1 egg, well beaten for the egg wash

Pascal's Pumpkin
Cheesecake

2 packages (8 ounces each)
cream cheese, softened

½ cup granulated sugar

½ teaspoon natural vanilla extract

2 eggs

½ cup canned pumpkin puree

½ teaspoon ground cinnamon

dash ground cloves

dash ground nutmeg

1 prebaked 9" Almond Tart shell
(see page 81)

½ cup heavy cream, whipped
with 1 tablespoon granulated sugar

Pascal's Pumpkin Cheesecake

Gateau au Fromage Blanc et au Potiron

Rich with pumpkin and spice, and wrapped in a tender almond pastry, this cheesecake will add an extraordinary flavor to your evening. Guaranteed to please, this recipe is simple, unusual, and easy to put together. Why wait until Thanksgiving? Serve it for any Fall or Winter celebration and enjoy!

Using an electric mixer, combine the cream cheese, sugar, and vanilla extract until well blended. Blend in the eggs on medium speed. Do not overbeat. Remove one cup of the batter and set aside.

Add the pumpkin and the spices to the remaining batter and stir gently. Pour the cup of reserved batter into the piecrust then gently pour the pumpkin batter over the top.

Bake in a preheated 325° oven for 35 to 40 minutes, or until the center is almost set.

Cool to room temperature, then refrigerate for at least 3 hours. Top with freshly whipped cream before serving.

Serves 8

Potimarron is a favorite French pumpkin with a chestnut flavor

Almond Tart Dough

Pâte à tarte à l'Amande

This delicate crisp tart dough adds a lovely layer of toasty almond flavor to any fruit tart. It is simple to make, though a bit tricky to roll out. If you have trouble, use your fingers to gently and evenly press the pastry into the tarte shell — any imperfections will bake out. Use the scraps to make cookies, roll the scraps into a 1-inch log and chill for 1 hour. Cut ¼-inch disks from the log and bake in a preheated 350° oven for 10 minutes. They are delicious!

In a mixing bowl, combine the butter, sugar, egg, salt and vanilla until blended.

Sift the flour and mix with the almond meal. Add to the butter mixture. Do not over mix; stop when the dough is well combined. Wrap in plastic wrap and chill overnight, or at least 1 hour before use.

Divide the dough in half. Roll out one half at a time on a well floured surface to the desired size. Place the dough in a greased tart pan, prick the bottom of the shell with a fork or line with pie weights.

Bake in a preheated 350° oven for 25 minutes, or until golden brown.

Makes enough dough for a single 9-inch double crust pie or 2 tart shells

Almond Meal

Grind almonds in the food processor with the sugar until fine.

Almond Tart Dough

1 ½ sticks unsalted butter, softened

⅔ cup confectioners' sugar

1 large egg

½ teaspoon salt

½ teaspoon natural vanilla extract

2 ½ cups all purpose flour

¼ cup almond meal

Almond Meal

½ cups sliced almonds

1 tablespoon confectioners' sugar

Pecans can be substituted for almonds.

Brioche

2 tablespoons lukewarm water

1 teaspoon dry yeast

4 cups all purpose flour

¾ cup milk

1 ½ teaspoons salt

2 large eggs

¼ cup plus 3 tablespoons granulated sugar

1 teaspoon vanilla extract

½ cup unsalted butter, softened

Brioche

Brioche

In patisseries and boulangeries throughout France, brioches sit on shelves like puffy, golden queens of the realm. You must be in line at the bakery well before 9 a.m. if you want one because they are so highly sought after for Holiday breakfasts. If late, you are likely to find them all gone. With this variation of a traditional recipe, you will never need to stand in line. You will always be ready to serve warm Brioche for any Holiday breakfast with plenty of butter and fresh fruit jam.

Mix the lukewarm water with the yeast and set aside for 10 minutes.

Using an electric mixer fitted with the dough hook attachment, combine the flour, milk, yeast mixture, salt, eggs, ¼ cup sugar and vanilla. Mix at slow speed until the dough is well combined. Increase speed and mix until the dough is smooth and detaches from the sides of the bowl.

In a separate small bowl, combine the butter and remaining sugar until the mixture is smooth. Slowly add the butter mixture to the dough, about 2 tablespoons at a time. Mix until the butter is completely incorporated, and the dough is smooth and elastic, but not sticky. Form the dough into a ball, and place in a bowl. Cover with a damp towel. Set aside, in a warm dry place, until the dough has increased in volume, about 2 hours.

Remove the dough from the bowl, and divide into 4 equal portions. Form each portion into a ball. Place 2 balls per buttered 4x8-inch loaf pans. 1 ball at each end of the pan, leaving a space in the middle. Cover and let rise to the rim of the pan, about 2 hours, or until doubled in bulk. This results in 2 double-bumped loaves.

In a small bowl, whisk together the egg and water to make an egg wash. Lightly brush the top of the dough with the egg wash. Bake in a preheated 350° oven for 40 to 45 minutes, or until golden brown. When done brush the top with the softened butter, and let cool.

Makes 2 loaves

The dough can rest overnight in the refrigerator.

Poolish

2 ¼ cups spring water (75°)

¾ teaspoons compressed yeast

2 cups plus 2 tablespoons
unbleached white flour

Baguette Dough

1 cup spring water

¾ teaspoon compressed yeast

3 ¾ to 4 ¾ cups unbleached white flour

1 ½ tablespoons sea salt

Old World Baguette

Baguette à l'Ancienne

The baguette is the national symbol of France, the hallmark of all that is good and wonderful à la Française. This recipe produces a dense, crusty baguette, just the thing to accompany savory pâtes, flavorful cheese or a wonderful meal. It is easy, and well worth the time it takes. Make baguettes, find some delicious French cheese and take a culinary voyage to France!

Poolish

To make the poolish (starter) – allow 24 hours.

Combine the water and the yeast in a 6 quart bowl. Let stand 1 minute, then stir with a wooden spoon until the yeast dissolves. Add the flour, and stir to the consistency of a thick batter. Cover with a damp towel or plastic wrap, and put in a warm place (75° to 80°) for 24 hours.

Baguette Dough

Combine the water and yeast, mix until dissolved. Stir into the poolish and stir until the poolish breaks up. Add 1 cup of the flour and mix until well combined. Add the salt and all but 1 cup of the remaining flour to make a thick mass that is difficult to stir. Turn onto a well-floured surface. Knead, adding flour as necessary until the dough is soft and smooth. Since flours vary in quality, you may need to add part or all of the remaining flour to reach the right consistency.

Knead for 15 minutes or until a small amount of dough pulled from the mass springs back quickly. Shape the dough into a ball.

Lightly oil the mixing bowl and add the ball shaped dough. Cover with a damp towel and let it rise in a warm place for 4 hours, or until doubled in volume.

 To see an example of the perfect baguette, visit la Madeleine.

Old World Baguette (suite)

Baguette à l'e

Transfer the dough to a board, and divide into 6 portions. Knead briefly and flatten each portion with the heel of your hand, and shape each into a 14-inch baguette.

Place the baguettes seam side up on a well-floured towel. Cover with a damp towel and let proof for 2 hours in a warm place.

Preheat the oven to 450°, and place a baking stone in the center of the oven.

Using the towel as an aid, gently roll each loaf onto a lightly floured baking pan so that they sit seam side down. Using a very sharp knife score the loaves by making quick cuts ½ inch deep on the diagonal. Put the loaves on the baking stone in the oven. Spray the inner walls of the oven with cold water to create steam and close the door.

Bake in the preheated oven 20 to 25 minutes, or until golden brown.

Makes 6 Baguettes

Feuilletage Dough

½ stick butter, for beurre noisette

6 cups unbleached flour

1 teaspoon salt

1 ¾ cup water

4 sticks cold unsalted butter

Feuilletage Dough
Pâte Feuilletée

Feuilletage is one of the crown jewels of French pastry. Light and multi-layered, it is infinitely versatile. The recipe is lengthy but simple; the result is an impressive, shatteringly crisp and buttery flavored treat.

In a heavy saucepan, over medium heat, melt the ½ stick of butter until the butter is caramel color. This should take about 4 minutes and will give the butter a slight hazelnut flavor. Transfer the melted butter to another container and let it cool to room temperature.

In a mixing bowl, combine the flour, salt and beurre noisette. Add the water and mix until the dough forms a ball. Do not overmix, the dough will be quite rough at this point.

Cover with plastic wrap and let it rest for 1 hour in the refrigerator.

Lightly flour the butter and place between two sheets of waxed paper. Flatten the butter with a rolling pin. Fold and roll out the butter until it is the same consistency as the dough. Shape into a 4-inch square and flour it lightly.

Roll out the dough on a lightly floured surface, preferably cold, into a circle about 18 inches in diameter.

Put the butter in the center of the dough, and fold the sides over the butter. You will have basically enclosed the butter in a "package" of dough. Using a rolling pin, press gently on the ends to enclose the butter.

Turn the dough over and roll it out to form a 16-inch rectangle. Then fold the dough in three (that's called a single turn). Roll out and fold again. Cover with plastic wrap and refrigerate for 1 hour.

Roll and fold twice (2 turns), and let the dough rest in the refrigerator for 1 hour. Roll and fold (2 more turns) and then cover the dough with plastic wrap.

Depending upon the use of the dough, refer to the recipe for cutting and rolling directions.

Makes 4 pounds

Les Notes

Conversion Chart

U.S. Weights & Measures

1 pinch = less than 1/8 teaspoon (dry)

1 dash = 3 drops to 1/4 teaspoon (liquid)

3 teaspoons = 1 tablespoon = 1/2 ounce (liquid and dry)

2 tablespoons = 1 ounce (liquid and dry)

4 tablespoons = 2 ounces (liquid and dry) = 1/4 cup

5 1/3 tablespoons = 1/3 cup

16 tablespoons = 48 teaspoons

32 tablespoons = 16 ounces = 2 cups = 1 pound

64 tablespoons = 32 ounces = 1 quart = 2 pounds

1 cup = 8 ounces (liquid) = 1/2 pint

2 cups = 16 ounces (liquid) = 1 pint

4 cups = 32 ounces (liquid) = 2 pints = 1 quart

16 cups = 128 ounces (liquid) = 4 quarts = 1 gallon

1 quart = 2 pints (dry)

8 quarts = 1 peck (dry)

4 pecks - 1 bushel (dry)

Approximate Equivalents

1 quart (liquid) = about 1 litre

8 tablespoons = 4 ounces = 1/2 cup = 1 stick butter

1 cup all-purpose presifted flour = 5 ounces

1 cup stoneground yellow cornmeal = 4 1/2 ounces

1 cup granulated sugar = 8 ounces

1 cup brown sugar = 6 ounces

1 cup confectioners' sugar = 4 1/2 ounces

1 large egg = 2 ounces = 1/4 cup = 4 tablespoons

1 egg yolk = 1 tablespoon + 1 teaspoon

1 egg white = 2 tablespoons + 2 teaspoons

Conversion Chart (suite)

Temperatures:

° Fahrenheit (F) to ° Celcius (C)

-10°F	=	-23.3°C (freezer storage)
0°F	=	-17.7°C
32°F	=	0°C (water freezes)
50°F	=	10°C
68°F	=	20°C (room temperature)
100°F	=	37.7°C
150°F	=	65.5°C
205°F	=	96.1°C (water simmers)
212°F	=	100°C (water boils)
300°F	=	148.8°C
325°F	=	162.8°C
350°F	=	177°C (baking)
375°F	=	190.5°C
400°F	=	204.4°C (hot oven)
425°F	=	218.3°C
450°F	=	232°C (very hot oven)
475°F	=	246.1°C
500°F	=	260°C (broiling)

Conversion Factors

If you need to convert measurements into their equivalents in another system, here's how to do it:

Weight

ounces to grams:	ounce x 28.3 = grams
grams to ounces:	gram x 0.0353 = ounces
pounds to grams:	pound x 453.59 = grams
pounds to kilograms:	pound x 0.45 = kilograms

Liquid Measures

ounces to milliliters:	ounce x 30 = milliliters
cups to liters:	cup x 0.24 = liters

Temperatures

Fahrenheit (°F) to Celsius (°C): $[(F - 32) \times 5] \div 9 = C$
Celsius (°C) to Fahrenheit (°F): $[(C \times 9) \div 5] + 32 = F$

Dimensions

inches to centimeters:	inch x 2.54 = centimeters
centimeters to inches:	centimeter x 0.39 = inches

Glossary

Almond Meal	almonds ground with sugar into a fine powder
Aspic	a savory jelly made from beef, fish or vegetable stock and gelatin
Baking Stone	an unglazed quarry tile about ½-inch thick, used as a surface for baking breads and pizzas because of its ability to retain heat and produce exceptional crusts
Balsamic Vinegar	a sweet-tart vinegar made from the unfermented juice of the Trebbiano grape found only around Modena, Italy and aged for at least six years
Baguette	a long cylindrical French loaf with a crisp brown crust and a chewy interior
Baton	a small stick shaped pastry
Beurre Blanc	a thick smooth sauce made from vinegar, white wine and shallots and chilled butter, often used as a sauce for fish
Beurre d'Escargot	compound butter with garlic and parsley used to stuff snails
Beurre Noisette	butter heated gently until it becomes hazelnut in color and taste
Blanched Almonds	almonds plunged into boiling water for a short time; done to make it easier to remove the skin
Bolete	a wild mushroom, also called porcini
Boursin	a triple cream cheese flavored with herbs, pepper or garlic
Bread Flour	a high gluten blend of hard wheat flour, malted barley and Vitamin C
Brioche	light yeast bread made with butter and eggs
Butter Cream	an uncooked frosting made from confectioners' sugar, butter, eggs and cream
Candied Fruit	fruits that have been preserved in sugar, including cherries, oranges and apricots
Caramelize	to dissolve sugar and water over heat until it turns golden brown
Celery Root	also known as celeriac; a brown, knobby winter vegetable that tastes like a cross between celery and parsley
Chambord	a raspberry liqueur

Chanterelle	a trumpet-shaped, wild mushroom known for its delicate flavor
Charlotte	a popular French cake made by lining a mold with ladyfingers or génoise and filling it with a flavored cream
Charlotte Mold	a bucket-shaped mold made of tinned-steel and used to bake custards, puddings and traditional French charlottes
Cornichon	a small, tart pickle traditionally used as an accompaniment for paté
Crème Anglaise	a delicate rich custard sauce made of egg yolks and sweetened milk
Crème Frâiche	a thickened heavy cream with a nutty flavor, to make crème frâiche, combine 1 cup heavy cream with 2 tablespoons buttermilk. Mix well and let sit for at least 16 hours at room temperature. Stir and refrigerate until ready to use.
Crouton	bread that has been baked or sautéed with garlic and herbs
Darioles	small chocolate cake with a molten middle
Deglaze	to add broth, wine or water to a pan in which food has been cooked, stirring and scraping to dissolve the browned bits from the bottom of the pan
Dredge	to coat food with a mixture, usually flour, salt and pepper, before sautéing or pan-frying
Duxelle	a mixture of finely chopped and cooked mushrooms, herbs and shallots; used as a filling
Egg Wash	a mixture of egg and water or egg and milk brushed over baked goods before baking to give a glossy sheen
Emulsify	to mix ingredients, usually oil and vinegar, until they do not separate
Foie Gras	liver of a goose or duck, which has been fattened by force-feeding
Feuilletage	puff pastry; flaky, buttery dough, which separates into paper-thin layers as it bakes and expands
Ganache	a chocolate filling, often enriched with cream, liqueur and flavorings
Génoise	a traditional French sponge cake that is used as a base for many elaborate pastry creations
Goat Cheese	in French, chèvre; cheese made from goat's milk, including Montrachet and Bucheron
Gooseberry	a small, sour berry used for jams and pies as well as in sauces for game
Grand Marnier	one of France's most renowned liqueurs, made from the dried peel of the green oranges of the West Indies
Gratin	sauced food baked in the oven and topped with cheese or breadcrumbs
Gruyère	a French cheese also known as Franche-Comté made from unpasturized cow's milk; known for its smooth flavor and nutty finish

Half-and-Half	equal parts of light cream and milk
Haricots Verts	very thin green beans, especially popular and common in France
Knead	to press dough with hands, folding and refolding, to make it elastic and smooth
Ladyfinger	a light, airy cookie shaped like a finger used as an accompaniment to desserts or to line a charlotte mold
Lavender Honey	honey made from lavender flowers
Macerate	to put food in a liquid to tenderize and absorb flavor, especially fruits
Miche	a large round loaf of bread
Mignonette Sauce	a classic French sauce made with vinegar, shallots, salt, pepper and sometimes lemon zest
Mirepoix	a mixture of diced carrots, onions, celery and herbs sauteed in butter, sometimes bacon or ham is added
Parchment Paper	a specially developed grease and moisture resistant paper used to line pans before baking
Pastis	an anise-flavored spirit popular along the Mediterranean
Pastry Bag	a reinforced bag rolled into a conical shape and holding a small stainless-steel cone at the tip; filled with icing and then squeezed to decorate cakes and pastries
Pesto	an uncooked sauce made by puréeing herbs or greens with garlic, nuts, salt and dry, sharp cheese and then emulsified with olive oil
Pith	the soft white layer between the outer peel and the flesh of citrus fruit
Proof	dissolve yeast in warm water till it bubbles, tests that the yeast is alive
Reduce	to thicken a sauce by boiling down, which reduces the volume and intensifies the flavor
Rock Lobster	in French, langouste; a variety of lobster with no front claw
Royal Icing	a sweet, stiff meringue of egg white and powdered sugar used to decorate cakes
Sauté	to cook food quickly in a small amount of oil over direct heat
Scald	to cook a liquid over low heat just until it reaches the boiling point
Sear	to brown the surface of meat quickly in a pan over high heat so that juices are sealed in
Sea Salt	evaporated crystals from seawater; sea salt is said to be purer than table salt since it contains no additives
Shallot	a small type of onion tinged with the flavor of garlic

Sherry Vinegar	vinegar made with sherry and allowed to age for three to four months
Shucked Oysters	fresh oysters (bivalves) removed from the shell
Star Anise	a star-shaped seed pod with a licorice flavor
Stock	a long-simmering broth made from meat, poultry, fish or vegetables with the addition of herbs and spices; used as the basis for many soups
Tapenade	a thick paste made from olives, capers, anchovies and lemon juice
Tart Shell	a freestanding mold or shell used to hold pie or quiche filling; some recipes call for pre-baked; i.e., baked with pie weights in it and removed before filling is added
Temper	to cool an ingredient before adding it to a hot one
Vanilla Bean	the seedpod of a tropical orchid used in flavoring, especially desserts
Vinaigrette	a basic oil and vinegar combination used to dress salads and other cold dishes
Zest	outermost exterior peel of citrus fruit, usually orange or lemon

Index